EZRA, NEHEMIAH, AND ESTHER

STUDENT
GENESIS TO REVELATION SERIES
BOOK 7

ABINGDON PRESS
Nashville

TABLE OF CONTENTS

Now these are the people of the province who . . .
returned to Jerusalem and Judah, each to his own town (2:1).

— 1 —

The Exiles Return

Ezra 1–2

Although little known to most Christians today, Ezra was quite prominent in his own day. There is a growing consensus among Old Testament scholars that Ezra wrote not only the book that bears his name, but First and Second Chronicles and Nehemiah as well. Some believe he was responsible for the final editing of the entire Old Testament. Two books in the Apocrypha claim Esdras (the Greek form of *Ezra*) as their author. And the book, The Revelation of Ezra, also purports to be by him. He is referred to often by the Jewish historian Josephus, a younger contemporary of the apostle Paul. His praises are sung in the Talmud, a collection of teachings supplementing and interpreting the Hebrew Scriptures. Ezra is commonly called the father (or sometimes the second father) of Judaism. We are dealing, then, with a man of no mean stature.

The Book of Ezra does not mention the man Ezra until Chapter 7. The first six chapters provide a history of the Hebrew people from the time Cyrus issued his edict in 538 B.C. to the completion of the second temple, about 515 B.C.

DIMENSION ONE:
WHAT DOES THE BIBLE SAY?

Answer these questions by reading Ezra 1

1. What Persian king makes a proclamation? (1:1)

2. What does Cyrus say God wants him to do? (1:2)

3. What does Cyrus allow the people of God to do? (1:3)

4. What does Cyrus say the Jews who remain in Persia are to do? (1:4)

5. Who rises up to return to Jerusalem? (1:5)

6. What do those not going to Jerusalem give to aid those who are going? (1:6)

7. What does Cyrus bring out to give to those returning to Jerusalem? (1:7)

8. To whom does Cyrus have Mithredath give these vessels? (1:8)

Answer these questions by reading Ezra 2

9. Where do the people go when they return to Judah? (2:1)

10. What category of people does Ezra enumerate first? (2:2)

11. What group of people does Ezra enumerate next? (2:36)

12. What is the third group Ezra enumerates? (2:40)

13. What other groups does Ezra list? (2:41, 42, 43, 55)

14. What is different about the people Ezra mentions next? (2:59)

15. What happens to those who claim to be sons of the priests, but cannot prove they are? (2:61-62)

16. The governor says these priests may eat the holy food when? (2:63)

17. Why do some of the heads of families make freewill offerings? (2:68)

DIMENSION TWO:
WHAT DOES THE BIBLE MEAN?

Background Information on Ezra

The Book of Ezra begins with Cyrus, the king of Persia, issuing a proclamation allowing all Jews to return to Jerusalem to rebuild their temple. Three questions come to mind immediately. Who was Cyrus? Where were the Jews? Why did the Temple need to be rebuilt?

Cyrus had become king of Anshan in 559 B.C. He quickly put together alliances that gave him a dominant role in all of Persia. From there he marched westward and conquered the kingdoms of Asia Minor, all the way to the Aegean Sea. In 539 B.C., he conquered Nebuchadnezzar, king of Babylon, and the large Babylonian Empire. It was at this point that the Jews came under Cyrus's province. Back in 587 B.C., Nebuchadnezzar had conquered Judah, and made it part of the Babylonian Empire.

Nebuchadnezzar had left Jerusalem in ruins, razing both the palace and the Temple. He also had deported the Israelite leaders to the far corners of the empire. All of this was consistent with his belief that the surest way to keep his empire intact was to destroy both the government and the religion of the conquered people, and to deprive them of any leadership.

Cyrus's philosophy was different. He believed that people were more easily governed when they were happy. His policy, therefore, was to let conquered peoples remain in their own lands and worship their own gods. So in 538 B.C., in the twenty-first year of his reign, but still in the first year of his rule over all the kingdoms of the earth (Ezra 1:2), Cyrus issued the proclamation we read about in Ezra 1:1-4. This proclamation allowed the people to return to their native land and to rebuild their Temple.

❑ *Ezra 1:1-4.* The edict of Cyrus contains the following points: (1) any Jews who wish to do so may return to Jerusalem; (2) those who do return will be expected to rebuild the Temple; and (3) all Jews who do not return will be expected to give financial aid to those who do.

THE EXILES RETURN　　　　　　　　　　　　　　　**5**

❑ *Ezra 1:5.* The tribes of Judah and Benjamin were the two tribes that had remained loyal to the house of David when the nation split in 922 B.C. Northern Israel, composed of the other ten tribes, had fallen in 722 B.C. When Nebuchadnezzar conquered southern Judah in 587 B.C., he took the leaders he transported to Babylon from the tribes of Judah and Benjamin. The descendants of those leaders are the people now preparing to return to Jerusalem.

❑ *Ezra 1:7.* Nebuchadnezzar had plundered the costly vessels that were kept in the Temple (2 Kings 24:12-13; 25:13-15). Cyrus now returns these vessels.

❑ *Ezra 1:8.* Shesbazzar is called Shenazzar in 1 Chronicles 3:18. (People often use shortened or slightly altered names; Richie, Dick, or Ricky are nicknames for Richard; and Liz, Beth, or Betty are short for Elizabeth.) He was a son of King Jehoiachin, and is therefore called the prince of Judah.

❑ *Ezra 1:9-11.* Notice the large number of vessels that Cyrus returns to the Jews and the expensive metals of which they are made.

❑ *Ezra 2:1.* When the Bible says the captives returned "each to his own town," it is not clear whether it means they returned to the towns where they had lived before the Exile or the towns where they lived at the time Ezra wrote, about one hundred years later.

❑ *Ezra 2:2-35.* The first list given is of "the men of the people of Israel," that is, the laity as distinguished from the priests. Some are listed as "descendants of" different persons. Others are listed as "the men of" certain places. These persons are listed not by families, but by towns.

❑ *Ezra 2:36-39.* The number of priests is 4,289. That number seems unusually large, since it is about one in ten for the entire group.

❑ *Ezra 2:38.* Pashur was the priest who put Jeremiah in the stocks (Jeremiah 20:1-16).

❑ *Ezra 2:39.* The name *Harim* means *dedicated.*

❑ *Ezra 2:40.* The Levites were assistants to the priests. The number of Levites returning from Babylon to Jerusalem is unusually small, only seventy-four, the smallest of all the groups. The reasons for this may well be due to the fact that their services were not needed during the Exile, since there was no Jewish temple in Babylon, and the Levites were forced to seek secular employment. Also, the Levites may have been mistreated during the Exile (Nehemiah 13:10).

❑ *Ezra 2:41.* The singers were the persons who sang during temple services.

❑ *Ezra 2:42.* The gatekeepers were those who guarded the gates on all four sides of the temple complex (1 Chronicles 9:23-24).

❑ *Ezra 2:43.* The temple servants were set apart by Moses (Numbers 31:30, 47) and later by David (Ezra 8:20) to assist the Levites in the Temple.

❑ *Ezra 2:55.* Solomon's servants are mentioned in the Bible here, in the corresponding list in Nehemiah 7:57-60, and again in Nehemiah 11:3. They are not mentioned anywhere else. These servants may have been captives of war. Or they may have been Israelites who permanently worked for the crown in exchange for the security of a place to sleep and food to eat.

❑ *Ezra 2:59-63.* Some of those who could not prove their descent and whether or not they belonged to Israel were lay persons, while others were priests. We are not told what restrictions were placed on the lay persons, but the priests were excluded from the priesthood until their ancestry could be proved.

❑ *Ezra 2:65.* The men and women singers mentioned here are different from the singers of verse 41. Only men sang in the temple services. These were singers who sang for the pleasure of the royal court (2 Samuel 19:35; 2 Chronicles 35:25; Ecclesiastes 2:8).

DIMENSION THREE:
WHAT DOES THE BIBLE MEAN TO ME?

Ezra 1:1—The Lord Stirred Up Cyrus

Ezra 1:1 says, "The LORD moved the heart of Cyrus." Yet Cyrus was a pagan king who worshiped a pagan god. Sometimes we hear persons say that God uses only Christians (sometimes it is said only born-again Christians) to do God's work in the world. Would the author of Ezra agree with that statement? Would you? Why or why not?

Ezra 1:3—The Long Journey

The trip back to Jerusalem was a long one and a hard one. It took a great deal of daring and courage and sacrifice on the part of those who returned. As we think about that, we cannot help but ask ourselves how willing we are to make such a sacrifice today. Jesus said we had to be willing to lose our lives for the sake of the gospel (Matthew 16:24-25; Mark 8:34-35; Luke 9:23-24). But do we really believe that? Are we willing to act on it? What kinds of sacrifice would such a commitment require of us?

Ezra 2:59-63—The Purity of Heritage

The emphasis the returned community placed on purity of heritage is shown in this section. These verses list by name the persons who could not prove that they were sons of Israel by direct descent. These persons were pronounced unclean and excluded from the priesthood.

How important is such purity of heritage for the church today? How exclusive or inclusive is your church? What factors account for the character of your particular church?

*And all the people gave a great shout of praise
to the LORD, because the foundation of the house
of the LORD was laid (3:11).*

— 2 —
Rebuilding the Temple
Ezra 3–4

DIMENSION ONE:
WHAT DOES THE BIBLE SAY?

Answer these questions by reading Ezra 3

1. When do the Israelites gather in Jerusalem? (3:1)

2. Who directs the people in building the altar? (3:2)

3. Whom do the people of Israel fear? (3:3)

4. What offerings and sacrifices do the people offer? (3:3-5)

5. Are the people able to offer their sacrifices to the Lord before the Temple is completed? (3:6)

6. From where do Jeshua and Zerubbabel have cedar trees brought for the construction of the Temple? (3:7)

7. When does the work on the Temple begin? (3:8)

8. What persons are appointed to have oversight of the work on the Temple? (3:8)

9. What do the priests, the Levites, and the people do after the foundation of the Temple has been laid? (3:10-11)

10. Who weeps while others are shouting for joy? (3:12)

Answer these questions by reading Ezra 4

11. Who approaches Zerubbabel and offers to help build the Temple? (4:1-2)

12. Why do the enemies say they want to help build the Temple? (4:2)

13. Is the offer accepted? (4:3)

14. What do the people of the land do next? (4:4-5)

15. What else do the people around the Israelites do to frustrate the people of Judah? (4:6)

16. What do the enemies do during the reign of Artaxerxes? (4:7)

17. What does the letter say? (4:12)

18. What will happen if the people are allowed to finish building Jerusalem? (4:13)

19. What proof of the accusations does the letter offer? (4:15)

20. What does Artaxerxes find when he searches the records? (4:17-19)

21. What does the king do then? (4:21)

22. What do the enemies do when they receive the letter from Artaxerxes? (4:23)

23. When does work on the Temple begin again? (4:24)

DIMENSION TWO: WHAT DOES THE BIBLE MEAN?

Ezra 3 and 4 describes the institution of the religious ceremonies in Jerusalem after the return from exile and the first attempts at rebuilding the Temple.

❏ *Ezra 3:1-2.* The seventh month is a month of religious significance for the Jews. When this month arrives, therefore, Jeshua and Zerubbabel and the people assemble in Jerusalem to build the altar of the God of Israel, and to offer burnt offerings upon it.

Notice that Jeshua is mentioned here before Zerubbabel. In every other instance where they are named together, Zerubbabel's name precedes that of Jeshua (Ezra 2:2; 3:8; 4:3; 5:2; Nehemiah 12:1; Haggai 1:1, 12, 14; 2:2, 4). Here we are dealing with the building of the altar and the offering of sacrifices. Therefore, Jeshua the priest would be of more significance than Zerubbabel the governor.

Apparently the people who remained after the destruction of Jerusalem had continued to worship in the ruins of the Temple (Jeremiah 41:5). Such worship would require an altar and an altar probably was built out of the Temple ruins. However, Ezra emphasizes that the altar constructed by Jeshua and Zerubbabel was built according to the instructions written in the law of Moses. This emphasis on the law of Moses continues in verses 4-5.

❏ *Ezra 3:3.* There is some confusion here. The returned exiles set the altar in its place "despite their fear of the peoples around them." One understanding of this phrase would be that the people hastily erect an altar so God will aid them in their conflict with the peoples of the lands. Another understanding would be that the people overcome the paralysis of fear to set up an altar in the face of potential enemies. However, in Chapter 4, the peoples of the lands come to Jerusalem and make a friendly offer to help build the Temple. Why, therefore, do the Israelites fear these people?

We do not possess the original manuscripts of any of the books of the Bible. What we have are copies made over many hundreds of years. Many times errors have slipped into the text, or even deliberate changes were made. Knowing which reading is the most accurate is not always possible. Therefore, a comparison of the various readings is often quite helpful.

In trying to understand verse 3, it is helpful to look at a different reading of this verse. Another manuscript states that people from other nations of the land were well disposed toward the altar. They aided the Israelites and offered sacrifices at the proper season and offered burnt offerings to the Lord. According to that version, then, the peoples of the lands come in friendship and help the returned exiles build their altar.

❏ *Ezra 3:4.* The Feast of Tabernacles seems to be the first religious festival the Israelites institute after they return to the Promised Land. The feast was adapted from a similar feast practiced by the people of Shechem and began as a joyous festival to celebrate the harvesting of the crops. (The Feast of Harvest referred to in Exodus 23:16 is the same feast.) Later the festival was lengthened to eight days and became not so much a celebration as a solemn occasion for the offering of sacrifices to God (Leviticus 23:33-43; Numbers 29:12-40).

❏ *Ezra 3:4-5.* Notice the continuation of the emphasis of verse 2 on the law of Moses. The phrases *in accordance with what is written, they celebrated the Feast of Tabernacles with the required number of burnt offerings prescribed for each day,* and *all the appointed sacred feasts* all refer to instructions given in the law.

❏ *Ezra 3:7.* The cedar trees from Lebanon are used because of their height, girth, strength, and straightness. They were regarded as the finest building trees available anywhere and were used by all the kingdoms of that area.

❏ *Ezra 3:8.* Notice that this verse speaks of "their arrival at the house of God," but at this time the house of God was not there. Ezra must have considered even the ruins of the old Temple as the house of God.

If you find this sentence difficult to understand, the fault is not yours! Actually this is an incomplete sentence. We are told Zerubbabel and Jeshua began something, but we are not told what they began to do. The NIV smoothes over the grammar somewhat by translating it "began the work." It is obvious from the context that what they began was the work on the Temple, but we are not told that in this sentence fragment.

The Levites who are twenty years old or older are given the responsibility of overseeing the work on the Temple.

❏ *Ezra 3:10-13.* When the foundation of the Temple is laid, a great celebration takes place. We might think of it as similar to our modern cornerstone ceremonies.

The poem quoted in verse 11 is from Psalm 136. Notice there the repeated refrain in every verse. The chronicler quotes this same poem in 1 Chronicles 16:34; 2 Chronicles 5:13; 7:3; and 20:21. The words also appear in Psalm 106:1; 107:1; and 118:1-4; and are quoted in Jeremiah 33:11.

Weeping is mingled with the great shout for joy. Many of the priests and Levites and old men who had seen the first Temple weep. Each is so loud that the people cannot distinguish the joyful shout from the people's weeping.

❏ *Ezra 4:1-3.* When the Samaritans hear that the returned exiles are building a temple to the Lord, they offer to help. After all, they say, "Like you, we seek your God and have been sacrificing to him since the time of Esarhaddon." But Zerubbabel and Jeshua refuse their offer. "You have no part with us in building a temple to our God," they say.

❏ *Ezra 4:4-5.* The Samaritans then retaliate by trying to keep them from building a temple, "during the entire reign of Cyrus . . . and down to the reign of Darius."

❏ *Ezra 4:6-24.* This section continues the idea of the Samaritans frustrating the work of the people of Judah "until the second year of the reign of Darius king of Persia." This story is chronologically out of place. Ahasuerus and Artaxerxes both come after Darius, not before. They are, in fact, his son and grandson, respectively. Samaritan opposition before the reign of Darius came during the reigns of Cyrus (539-530 B.C.) and Cambyses (530-522 B.C.). Perhaps the passage is simply meant to show that this is the kind of behavior Jews have always had to put up with from the Samaritans.

❏ *Ezra 4:7-16.* The letter (or letters) to Artaxerxes is a part of the section that is chronologically out of place. However, proof that the letter belongs during the reign of Artaxerxes is the fact that the letter deals with the rebuilding of the city walls. No mention is made in the letter of the rebuilding of the Temple, which was an important issue during the days of Cyrus and Cambyses.

As our text now stands, two letters are sent to Artaxerxes, one by Bishlam and Mithredath and Tabeel (verse 7), and one by Rehum and Shimshai (verse 8). The book of First Esdras (in the Apocrypha) reports only one letter, written by all five (1 Esdras 2:16). Possibly two letters were sent and the king ignored the first letter and took the matter seriously only after receiving a letter from Rehum the commander.

The letter says three things. First, it says that the Jews are "rebuilding that rebellious and wicked city" of Jerusalem. Second, if the Jews are allowed to finish rebuilding Jerusalem and its walls, the Jewish people will pay "no more taxes, tribute or duty," and therefore "the royal revenues will suffer." And third, if Artaxerxes will search the records of his fathers, he will discover that "this city is a rebellious city, troublesome to kings." In fact, that is why the city was destroyed to begin with.

❏ *Ezra 4:17-22.* The king sends an answer to Rehum and Shimshai. Search has been made, he says, and what you say about this city is true. The king therefore orders that these men stop and this city not be rebuilt until he issues an order to the contrary.

❏ *Ezra 4:23-24.* The king's letter is exactly what Rehum and Shimshai had hoped for. They hurry to Jerusalem and compel the Jews to stop work on the Temple. And so "until the second year of the reign of Darius king of Persia" the Temple is left uncompleted.

DIMENSION THREE:
WHAT DOES THE BIBLE MEAN TO ME?

Ezra 3:1—One in the Spirit

When the time came to build the altar, the people of Judah gathered in Jerusalem "as one man." It is not often that we in the church show that kind of unity today, is it? But sometimes it does happen. Can you think of a time when the men and women of your congregation gathered as one person? If so, what was the occasion? Why is it so hard to get church people to stand together on the great moral issues of the day?

Ezra 3:2—Who Is a Man or Woman of God?

Moses is called here "the man of God." What do you think the writer meant by that designation? Was Moses a person of God because he had been called by God (Exodus 3:1-10)? Because he had been obedient to God? Why?

Are there any men or women of God today? If so, who are they? Do they know any? Are there any in your own congregation or community? How many can you name? What makes them men or women of God?

Ezra 1-3—How Would You Feel?

Think back over the story we have read so far—Cyrus issues the decree allowing the Jews to return home; they come home to find the Temple in ruins; they begin rebuilding and celebrate when the foundation is completed; then the work is stopped until the second year of the reign of Darius. Try to imagine yourself in each of these situations. What emotions would you feel in each step along the way?

King Cyrus issued a decree to rebuild
this house of God (5:13).

—— 3 ——
The Decree of Cyrus
Ezra 5–6

DIMENSION ONE:
WHAT DOES THE BIBLE SAY?

Answer these questions by reading Ezra 5

1. What prophets inspire the people to resume work on the Temple? (5:1-2)

2. Who tries to make the people stop working on the Temple? (5:3-5)

3. To whom do Tattenai and Shethar-Bozenai write? (5:6)

4. What does their report say? (5:8)

5. Who issued a decree ordering the rebuilding of the Temple? (5:13)

6. What do Tattenai and Shethar-Bozenai ask the king to do? (5:17)

Answer these questions by reading Ezra 6

7. When Darius makes a search, what does he find? (6:1-5)

8. What does Darius command Tattenai and Shethar-Bozenai to do? (6:7)

9. What further decree does Darius make? (6:8-12)

10. When do the workmen finish the Temple? (6:15)

11. What do the people of Israel do when the Temple is completed? (6:16-18)

12. When do the Jews celebrate the Passover? (6:19)

13. Who is allowed to eat the Passover lamb? (6:19-21)

14. What emotions do the Jewish people have at this time? (6:22)

DIMENSION TWO: WHAT DOES THE BIBLE MEAN?

We noticed in the last lesson that part of the material in Chapter 4 is out of place. Verses 6-24 belong during the reigns of Ahasuerus and Artaxerxes rather than during the reigns of Cyrus and Cambyses. With the beginning of Chapter 5, and continuing through 6:18, we have the rest of the story left hanging at 4:5. Haggai and Zechariah fire the people up to resume work on the Temple (5:1-2). Tattenai and Shethar-Bozenai investigate the rebuilding activity and write to King Darius asking him what to do about it (5:3-17). Darius gives his full support to the building of the Temple, the Temple is completed, and the priesthood begins functioning once again (6:1-18). Chapter 6 closes with the people celebrating the Feast of Passover and Unleavened Bread (6:19-22).

❑ *Ezra 5:1-2.* The prophets Haggai and Zechariah, apparently disturbed because the work on the Temple had been abandoned, prophesied to the Jews in the name of the God of Israel. What they said is not recorded, but they seem to have spoken the right words. Zerubbabel and Jeshua were inspired and began to rebuild the Temple.

❑ *Ezra 5:3- 4.* Tattenai and Shethar-Bozenai and their associates apparently are making a routine check when they interrogate the workers. Remember that we are just in the second year of Darius's reign (4:24). It would be quite natural for the king to have his officers check the activities of all the people in his new kingdom. The officers ask the people of Israel by whose authority they are building a temple. They also demand a list of the workmen. Perhaps this was the original reason for compiling the list given in Chapter 2. This seems unlikely, however, since the Jews would have had an interest in the list whether or not they had had to compile it for Tattenai and his associates.

❑ *Ezra 5:5.* The Jews are not required to stop work on the Temple while Tattenai and Shethar-Bozenai await instructions from Darius. The author of Ezra attributes this good fortune to the providence of God.

❑ *Ezra 5:7-17.* Tattenai and Shethar-Bozenai report to Darius that they had inquired of the Jews who had granted them permission to rebuild the Temple. The Jews had answered, they tell Darius, by saying the Temple had been built a long time ago, but that Nebuchadnezzar had destroyed it and taken the people captive. But then, in the first year of Cyrus the king, Cyrus had decreed that the Temple should be rebuilt. Furthermore, said Cyrus, the gold and silver vessels that had been taken from the Temple should be returned to the Jews. Sheshbazzar then laid the foundations to the Temple, and it has been under construction "from that day to the present."

Having written all this to Darius, Tattenai and Shethar-Bozenai now say, "If it pleases the king, let a search be made in the royal archives . . . to see if King Cyrus did in fact issue a decree." They close by asking the king to tell them what he wants them to do.

❑ *Ezra 6:1-2.* King Darius follows the suggestion of Tattenai and Shethar-Bozenai. A search is made and the decree of Cyrus is found, not at Babylon where Tattenai and Shethar-Bozenai had suggested looking, but at Ecbatana, the summer palace. The fact that Darius has a search made at both Babylon and Ecbatana shows the importance he attaches to finding the decree.

In all the excavations that have been carried on in Babylon, none has uncovered a house of the archives there. It is not certain, therefore, that one ever existed. Perhaps "of Babylon"

(5:17) should read "at Babylon" (as in 6:1). If so, Ecbatana may have been the only place Darius looked.

❑ *Ezra 6:3-5.* The decree of Cyrus given here is the Aramaic form of the same decree given in Hebrew in Ezra 1:2-4. The two decrees are similar, but vary in the following ways:

1. The present decree does not give God the credit for the victories of Cyrus (compare 1:2).

2. Cyrus does not say in this decree that God "appointed me to build a temple for him at Jerusalem" (compare 1:2). He simply orders that the Temple be rebuilt (6:3).

3. Nothing in the present decree mentions letting the people return to Jerusalem from Babylon (compare 1:3).

4. Nothing in this decree mentions that those remaining in Babylon should give financial aid to those going back to rebuild the Temple (compare 1:4).

5. The dimensions of the Temple are given here, but not in the earlier decree (6:3).

6. The earlier decree does not mention that the cost of the rebuilding is to be borne by the royal treasury (compare 6:4).

7. The earlier decree does not mention the returning of the vessels that Nebuchadnezzar had taken from the Temple (6:5).

❑ *Ezra 6:6-12.* Darius rules that the edict by Cyrus should be enforced. He commands Tattenai and Shethar-Bozenai that they should keep away from the workers, and "do not interfere with the work on this temple of God." Moreover, Darius rules that the cost of rebuilding the Temple will be paid from the royal revenue. Also, whatever is needed for the daily sacrifices is to be "given them daily without fail." Then Darius tells why he is so interested that the sacrifices be continued—"that they may offer sacrifices pleasing to the God of heaven, and *pray for the well-being of the king* and his sons" (italics added). The Hebrew God was not his god, but Darius was not adverse to seeking help from all the gods he could! Darius ends the letter by decreeing that anyone who alters his edict will be dealt with severely.

Comparing this correspondence with Darius to the correspondence reported earlier with Artaxerxes (4:11-22) is interesting. In both cases, the Jews are engaged in building and the

Persian officials write to the king to ask what to do. In both cases, the officials suggest to the king that a search be made, in one case to verify what they have told the king, and in the other case to ascertain whether or not what the Jews have told them is actually true. In both cases, the king makes the search and answers the letter from the officials. In one case, the king forbids the continuation of the building; in the other case, the king decrees that it shall continue and orders that it be supported through the royal treasury.

❏ *Ezra 6:13-15.* Tattenai and Shethar-Bozenai carry out the king's orders to the letter. Work on the Temple prospered, and the Temple was completed "on the third day of the month Adar, in the sixth year of the reign of King Darius." Adar was the twelfth month in the Babylonian calendar, and would correspond most closely in time with our months of later February and early March. The Temple was finished, then, in the early spring of 515 B.C.

Possibly the urgency that Haggai and Zechariah felt for completing the Temple was not purely religious. There was political unrest in Persia at this time, and hope ran high in Israel that they might once again be an independent nation ruled by the house of David. It was this dream that Haggai and Zechariah appealed to, and this dream spurred the people on.

❏ *Ezra 6:16-22.* The people celebrate the completion of the Temple and dedicate it with a full ceremony. The next month they celebrate the Passover as well as the Feast of Unleavened Bread.

The dedication of the Temple is patterned after the dedication of Solomon's temple, though it is much less grandiose in scale. Here one hundred bulls, two hundred rams, four hundred lambs, and twelve he-goats are sacrificed. But when Solomon's temple was dedicated, we are told that so many sheep and oxen were sacrificed that "they could not be recorded or counted" (1 Kings 8:5). Later in the account, however, their number is given as twenty-two thousand oxen and a hundred and twenty thousand sheep (1 Kings 8:63; 2 Chronicles 7:5).

DIMENSION THREE:
WHAT DOES THE BIBLE MEAN TO ME?

Ezra 5:1-2—How Important Is a Sanctuary?

How important was it, do you think, that the Israelite people rebuild the Temple? How important is it that we have a building to worship in today? Would it be better to use the money to feed the poor rather than to build a sanctuary? Why or why not? What light, if any, does Luke 21:5-6 throw on this question? What about Matthew 19:21? Matthew 26:6-13?

Ezra 6:6-12—Church and State

Darius decreed that money from the royal treasury should be used to rebuild the Temple and that whatever the priests needed for the daily sacrifices should be provided for them. Do you see this decree as good or bad? Why? Should the government help finance churches today? Why or why not? What light, if any, does Mark 12:17 shed on this question?

Ezra 6:13-15—Religion and Politics

Earlier discussion suggested that the urgency Haggai and Zechariah felt for rebuilding the Temple may have been politically as well as religiously inspired. Do you see such motivation as positive or negative? Why? What movements can you think of that have combined political and religious fervor? How has this combination affected the success or failure of these movements?

Ezra . . . . was a teacher well versed
in the Law of Moses (7:6).

— 4 —

Ezra the Scribe

Ezra 7–10

DIMENSION ONE:
WHAT DOES THE BIBLE SAY?

Answer these questions by reading Ezra 7

1. When does Ezra arrive in Jerusalem? (7:1-8)

2. What has Ezra set his heart to do? (7:10)

3. Where will the people of Israel get the money to buy the animals and grain for their sacrifices and offerings? (7:14-18)

4. What decree does Artaxerxes make to the treasurers in the province Trans-Euphrates? (7:21-23)

5. What else does Artaxerxes tell the treasurers? (7:24)

6. What decree does Artaxerxes give to Ezra? (7:25-26)

7. What is Ezra's response to the decree? (7:27-28)

Answer these questions by reading Ezra 8

8. Who does Ezra discover to be missing? (8:15)

9. What does Ezra do then? (8:16-17)

10. What does Ezra do after Iddo sends temple servants? (8:21)

11. Why is Ezra ashamed to ask the king for protection? (8:22)

12. What responsibility does Ezra give the leading priests? (8:24-29))

13. What do the people do after they reach Jerusalem? (8:33, 35, 36)

Answer these questions by reading Ezra 9

14. What sin have the people, the priests, and the Levites committed? (9:1-2)

15. What does Ezra do when he hears this? (9:3)

16. What does Ezra do after the evening sacrifice? (9:5)

Answer these questions by reading Ezra 10

17. What do the people do while Ezra prays? (10:1)

18. What does Shecaniah suggest to Ezra? (10:2-3)

19. What does Ezra do then? (10:5)

20. What do the people of Israel decide to do? (10:10-14)

DIMENSION TWO:
WHAT DOES THE BIBLE MEAN?

❑ *Ezra 7:1-6.* We are introduced for the first time to Ezra. Ezra is the son of Seraiah. *Seraiah* is a name associated with the priestly class. The high priest at the time of the fall of Jerusalem was so named (2 Kings 25:18-21). The name given to Seraiah at his birth indicates the hopes his parents had for him. He never quite made it. But his son, Ezra, whose name means *help* or *assistance,* rose to the top.

Ezra is described as "a teacher well versed in the Law of Moses." Where the NIV calls Ezra a "teacher," the NRSV translates the word as "scribe." Originally a scribe was the secretary of a king and a member of his royal court. It was the scribe's duty to record the king's edicts and the official history of the land during the king's reign. Later the term came to be used for anyone who served as a secretary (as in Jeremiah 36:32) and for all those whose primary task was writing.

In Judaism the term *scribe* was applied specifically to those who copied the sacred writings. To be skilled as a scribe, then, was to be a careful copier of the sacred text. But in the process of copying the text over and over, the scribe also became quite learned in the fine points of the law. By the time of Jesus a scribe was called a *lawyer.* We do not know for sure just what the office of scribe was at the time of Ezra. We suspect, however, that when the author describes Ezra he wants us to know that Ezra was very knowledgeable about the contents and meaning of the law.

We are told next that the king granted him all that he asked, but we are not told what he had asked the king for. Later in the chapter (verses 11-26), we are told of a letter from King Artaxerxes to Ezra, and this letter is probably in reply to all that Ezra asked. When Artaxerxes says, "the hand of the Lord . . . was upon" Ezra, he indicates that God acted favorably toward Ezra.

❑ *Ezra 7:7-10.* Ezra did not make the trip to Jerusalem alone. Priests and Levites, singers and gatekeepers, and temple servants as well as some of the people of Israel went with him. Notice that we find here the same categories of people that accompanied Sheshbazzar on the first trip back (Ezra 2). The trip took four months. They traveled about seven to eight miles a day to cover approximately nine hundred miles.

❏ *Ezra 7:11-26.* These verses contain the letter written by Artaxerxes and given to Ezra. The letter contains three sections. The first is composed of verses 12-20. In this section Ezra is authorized to go to Jerusalem to determine how scrupulously the people in Jerusalem and Judah are living by God's law. Ezra is also given instructions concerning the money he takes with him.

The second portion of Artaxerxes's letter (verses 21-24) is addressed to the treasurers in the province Trans-Euphrates. They are told to give Ezra whatever he needs for his work. They are also given the limits placed on the amount. They are notified further that they shall not impose any taxes upon Ezra and his coworkers in the Temple.

The third part of Artaxerxes's letter (verses 25-26) gives Ezra the authority to appoint magistrates and judges. These officials will make sure all the Israelites in the province Trans-Euphrates know the laws of God. Both God's laws and the king's law are to be strictly enforced.

❏ *Ezra 7:27-28.* Ezra is grateful not only that the king has decreed that the Temple should be rebuilt, but also that he has been selected as the one to carry out the king's orders. With his spirits soaring, he gathers together the leaders of the Israelite people living in Persia and sets out for Jerusalem.

❏ *Ezra 8:1-14.* Contrary to the list given in Chapter 2, the priests are listed first here. We know Gershom and Daniel are priests only because their ancestries are given. (Phinehas is a descendant of Aaron, and Ithamar is the youngest son of Aaron.) The lay persons are then named according to families. A total of 1,514 men are listed, including both priests and lay persons. Wives and children also make the trip, though we do not know how many. In addition, there are forty-one Levites and two hundred and twenty temple servants (verses 18-20).

❏ *Ezra 8:15-20.* Ezra assembles his company at the canal that runs to Ahava (Ah-hah-VAH). There is no known town by the name of Ahava. In verses 21 and 31 the canal itself (which probably links up with the Euphrates River), not a town, is named Ahava.

As Ezra counts those in his company, he discovers there are no Levites among them. He therefore sends men of insight to Iddo who resides at Casiphia. Neither Iddo nor Casiphia is known to us outside this one passage. Iddo is able to supply Ezra with a capable man, Sherebiah, along with eighteen of his sons and kinsmen. He also finds Hashabiah, Jeshaiah, and twenty of their kinsmen and sons. In addition, he sends Ezra two hundred and twenty temple servants.

❏ *Ezra 8:21-23.* Before Ezra leaves, he proclaims a fast so that they could humble themselves before God and seek a straight journey. A straight journey is a safe one without fear of ambush and without too many rugged hills to climb.

❏ *Ezra 8:24-30.* Ezra selects twelve of the leading priests and gives them the responsibility of safely transporting the silver and gold and the vessels. Only two of the priests are named, and both of them are named earlier as Levites, rather than priests (verses 15-20).

Ezra tells the priests that they are holy to God and the vessels are holy. To be holy to the Lord is to be set apart for God's use. Both the priests and the vessels, therefore, are holy (Leviticus 21:1, 6; Joshua 6:19; 2 Chronicles 23:6; Zechariah 14:20-21). By saying the silver and the gold are a freewill offering to the Lord, Ezra hoped to instill in the priests a sense of the awesome responsibility he has given to them.

❏ *Ezra 8:31-36.* Ezra and his company leave Persia, and arrive safely in Jerusalem. The treasures that were carried and guarded by the priests are taken to the Temple. They are then counted, and the amounts recorded. Sacrifices are offered in gratitude for the safe journey, and Ezra and his followers take the king's commissions to the satraps and governors of the province. The priest who received the treasures at the Temple was Meremoth, grandson of Hakkoz (Nehemiah 3:4). The sons of Hakkoz were among those priests who came to Jerusalem with Zerubbabel (Ezra 2:61), but were unable to prove their genealogies (2:59). So they were excluded from the priesthood as unclean (2:62). Apparently the genealogy was found, for only a highly regarded priest would receive the temple treasures.

❑ *Ezra 9:1-5.* Ezra is upset about intermarriage because God had chosen Israel to be a holy nation. To be holy is to be set apart, and to be a nation set apart is to be different from the other nations. The people of Israel, therefore, were not to make marriages with the other nations (Deuteronomy 7:1-6) so they could remain set apart. God had set Israel apart and had specifically required that the people not defile their seed. (The word translated *race* in 9:2 is really *seed.*) Marrying foreign people also almost certainly would lead to worshiping other gods. That had happened to Solomon (1 Kings 11:1-11), and it could happen again.

So when Ezra heard of these marriages, he tore his garments and pulled his hair from his head and beard. He tore his garments to express grief, sorrow, or utter dismay. Pulling hair from his head and beard had essentially the same meaning.

"At the evening sacrifice" may simply refer to the time of day. But Ezra probably chose this time because of the appropriateness of prayer at that hour. The practice of having specified times of the day for prayer was followed both in the Old Testament (Daniel 6:10) and the New Testament (Acts 3:1).

Ezra prays with his arms outspread and his palms facing up. This was a common posture for prayer (Exodus 9:29; 1 Kings 8:22) and may have been the posture of the Pharisee in Jesus' parable (Luke 18:11).

❑ *Ezra 9:6-15.* In this prayer Ezra confesses the guilt of his people, acknowledges God's grace in showing them his favor in spite of their great guilt, and asks (perhaps directing the question more to the people gathered around him than to God), "Shall we again break your commands? Would you not be angry enough with us to destroy us?"

Notice that Ezra speaks of "our sins" and "our guilt" (verse 6). He is not personally involved in the sins, but he so identifies himself with his people that their sin becomes his sin.

Ezra reveals a prophet's understanding of Israel's sufferings, when he explains that their kings and their priests have been given into the hand of the kings of the lands. This has happened because God has been punishing them for their sins.

God has shown favor and given the remnant (the returning Israelites) a secure hold in God's sanctuary (Jerusalem). God has given them steadfast love, says Ezra, through the kings of Persia (verse 9). God moved Cyrus to allow the remnant to return to Jerusalem and prompted Darius to allow Zerubbabel and Jeshua to repair the Temple. And God inspired Artaxerxes to allow Nehemiah and his workmen to give protection in Judea and Jerusalem (verse 9). Even after all that, says Ezra, again "we have disregarded the commands you gave."

❑ *Ezra 10:1-15.* While Ezra is praying, a large group of the faithful gather before him and weep. Then Shecaniah suggests they make a covenant with God to send away all these wives and children.

Notice that Shecaniah's name does not appear in verses 18-44 as one of the guilty. Yet he, like Ezra, identifies himself with the sinners. But it is considerably easier for one who did not have to send away his wife and children to make that suggestion.

Ezra spends the night in the chamber of Jehohanan. The next day he sends a proclamation to everyone to assemble at Jerusalem. If persons do not come within three days their property will be forfeited and they will be banned from the congregation. You will recognize these two punishments as two of the four powers given to Ezra by Artaxerxes (7:26).

The open square (verse 9) was a large area and a favorite spot for large assemblies. Ezra read the law there (Nehemiah 8:1). The people tremble because of the gravity of the matter and because of the heavy rain. The assembly takes place on the twentieth day of the ninth month, the month of Chislev, our month of December. That was the time of the beginning of the winter rains.

The response to Ezra's call for confession is amazing! The only concession the people ask for is that Ezra not try to get it all done at once. They propose a method and a timetable for getting the matter taken care of. Only four persons oppose the plan, and it is not clear whether they oppose the plan or the timetable.

❑ *Ezra 10:16-44.* Three months later, the men Ezra selects finish their work (verses 16-17). The author then lists the names and family heritage of all the guilty persons. No Jewish women are accused of marrying foreign men.

DIMENSION THREE:
WHAT DOES THE BIBLE MEAN TO ME?

Ezra 7:26—Civil Law and Religious Convictions

The magistrates and judges Ezra appointed were to bring punishment upon those who did not obey the laws of God and the king's laws. Yet these two sets of laws sometimes come into conflict. What are we to do then?

What are we to do when the laws of human beings seem to contradict the laws of God? What is the difference between a just law and an unjust law? Is civil disobedience a proper way to change laws? Why or why not?

Ezra 9-10—Exclusiveness Rears Its Ugly Head

Two whole chapters in this lesson deal with the issue of exclusiveness. Ezra was absolutely convinced that he was doing the right thing by having the Hebrew men send away their foreign wives and their children. But was he? Can the spirit of intolerance be worse than the danger of syncretism (the attempt to combine or reconcile differing or opposing points of view, especially in religion)? Why or why not? What advantages are there in having a church where everyone thinks alike? What are the dangers?

Ezra 9:6-15—Preaching a Sermon While Praying

When have you had the suspicion that your pastor was really preaching when he or she was leading the congregation in prayer? Does your pastor refer to God in the third person in times of prayer (saying "he" or "him" rather than "thou" or "you")? Do you use the third person when you pray? Are you talking *to* God or *about* God? If you are talking *about* God rather than *to* God, is that really prayer?

Ezra seems to have his audience in mind as he offers his prayer in the square in front of the Temple. His prayer is calculated to get a particular response from the people. That is the purpose of a sermon. Prayer is talking to God.

Is what Ezra doing legitimate? Is it all right to preach as you pray? Why or why not?

The words of Nehemiah
son of Hacaliah (1:1).

——— 5 ———
Nehemiah the Cupbearer
Nehemiah 1–2

DIMENSION ONE:
WHAT DOES THE BIBLE SAY?

Answer these questions by reading Nehemiah 1

1. Whom does Nehemiah ask about the Jews still living in Jerusalem? (1:2)

2. How do these men say the Jews in Jerusalem are doing? (1:3)

3. How does Nehemiah react to this news? (1:4)

4. What is Nehemiah's position in Persia? (1:11)

Answer these questions by reading Nehemiah 2

5. Who asks Nehemiah why he is sad? (2:2)

6. After hearing why Nehemiah is sad, what does the king ask Nehemiah? (2:4)

7. What does Nehemiah request? (2:5, 7-8)

8. Who is displeased that Nehemiah has come to help the people of Israel? (2:10)

9. What does Nehemiah do at night? (2:13-15)

10. What does Nehemiah say to the Israelite priests, nobles, and officials? (2:17-18)

11. What do the people say? (2:18)

12. What do Sanballat, Tobiah, and Geshem say to the Israelites? (2:19)

13. How does Nehemiah answer them? (2:20)

DIMENSION TWO: WHAT DOES THE BIBLE MEAN?

The Book of Ezra and the Book of Nehemiah originally formed one book. We already have seen that parts of Ezra are out of chronological sequence. A portion of the story of Ezra is in the Book of Nehemiah. In addition, we shall meet Nehemiah, struggle with him to get the city wall built, rejoice with him at the completion of the wall, and try to stay out of his way as he institutes his social and religious reforms. Nehemiah is a stern man, strict in his interpretation of the law, but also a very religious man, determined that he and all his people will follow the laws of God.

❏ *Nehemiah 1:1-4.* Like the Book of Ezra, the Book of Nehemiah begins its story in the kingdom of Persia (Ezra 1:1). Susa had been the capital of Elam (Ezra 4:9; Daniel 8:2), and became the capital of the Persian Empire (Esther 1:2, 5). Xenophon, a Greek historian who lived almost a century after Nehemiah, refers to Susa as the site of the king's winter palace.

Hanani, one of Nehemiah's brethren, comes to him with certain men from Judah. Nehemiah asks these men about the Jews who had escaped exile, and about Jerusalem. The Jews who had escaped exile are the descendants of those who had not been sent into exile at the time of the fall of Judah at the hands of Nebuchadnezzar (2 Kings 25:1-5, 11-12).

The men answer both of Nehemiah's questions. They tell him that the survivors are in great trouble, the wall of Jerusalem is broken down, and its gates have been destroyed. Nehemiah is devastated by this report. He weeps and mourns for days and prays before the God of heaven.

What had happened to cause this trouble? When was the wall broken down, and when were its gates destroyed by the fire? The men from Judah could have been referring to the destruction that happened at the hands of Nebuchadnezzar in 586 B.C. But surely Nehemiah already knew about that. Every Jew knew about that. It does not seem, then, that a report of this catastrophe that happened some 141 years earlier would have caused such distress for Nehemiah. What trouble then are the men of Judah talking about?

A delegation of Jews had left Persia earlier and had begun repairing the walls (Ezra 4:12). Bishlam, Mithredath, Tabeel, Rehum, and Shimshai had all written to Artaxerxes to try to put a stop to it. Artaxerxes had written back to his officials, saying, "Issue an order . . . to stop work, so that this city will not be rebuilt until I so order" (Ezra 4:21). Rehum and Shimshai then hurried to Jerusalem and by using force stopped the rebuilding. If Rehum and Shimshai were so eager to stop the rebuilding of the wall, they probably would also tear down the work that had already been done. And this may well be what the men of Judah report to Nehemiah. If so, we can understand why Nehemiah had not yet heard of it and why the news would cause him such grief.

❑ *Nehemiah 1:5-11.* These verses record Nehemiah's prayer. It has striking similarities to the prayer of Ezra recorded in Ezra 9:6-15. Both prayers confess the sins of the people, both now and in the past (Nehemiah 1:6-7; Ezra 9:6-7). Ezra and Nehemiah both identify with the guilty (Nehemiah 1:6-7; Ezra 9:6-7). Both prayers acknowledge that God gave the people plenty of warning and their punishment has been just and fair (Nehemiah 1:8; Ezra 9:10-15). Both prayers acknowledge God's grace (Nehemiah 1:9-10; Ezra 9:8-9, 13, 15). However, the prayers end on different notes. Nehemiah pleads for God's attention and favorable response (Nehemiah 1:11; compare 1:6), while Ezra says, "Here we are before you in our guilt, though because of it not one of us can stand in your presence" (Ezra 9:15).

❑ *Nehemiah 2:1-8.* A period of several months has elapsed since Nehemiah's prayer. Nehemiah is serving the king wine, unaware that his sadness is showing on his face. But Artaxerxes asks why Nehemiah is sad. This is the opportunity Nehemiah has been waiting for! Yet he is afraid to tell the king what is on his mind. He is afraid because Artaxerxes had been the one who had ordered that the rebuilding of the walls of Jerusalem be stopped (Ezra 4:23-24). How can Nehemiah now tell the king that what he wants him to do is to reverse his earlier stand and let the city be rebuilt?

But Nehemiah overcomes his fear and decides to risk it. He tells the king that the city of his fathers lies waste and its gates have been destroyed by fire. He must have rehearsed his speech because he says exactly the right words. Notice that the men of Judah had said, "The wall of Jerusalem is broken down" (1:3). Nehemiah does not say that. He does not mention Jerusalem by name at all. Earlier Artaxerxes had found that Jerusalem was a rebellious and seditious city (Ezra 4:19). So Nehemiah carefully avoids the name of the city. Rather, he refers to it as "the city where my fathers are buried." Persian religion emphasized honoring the dead, and Nehemiah undoubtedly knows that the king would be moved by such an appeal. Nor does Nehemiah mention the wall. He tells the king about the gates, but he does not mention the wall. Artaxerxes had stopped the work on the wall once; so Nehemiah wants to make his appeal without reminding the king of that.

The king finds Nehemiah's concern legitimate, and gives him permission to go to the city of his fathers and rebuild it. Nehemiah asks for letters from the king so the governors of the province Trans-Euphrates would allow him to pass through their territories, and so Asaph would give him timber. The king gives Nehemiah the letters, and Nehemiah recognizes the providence of God in all these doings.

❑ *Nehemiah 2:9-10.* The letters from Artaxerxes do not guarantee Nehemiah a trouble-free time to rebuild the city walls. As soon as he reaches Jerusalem, Sanballat and Tobiah begin giving him trouble.

Sanballat was the governor of Samaria and little is known about him. He has a Babylonian name, but many children were

EZRA, NEHEMIAH, AND ESTHER

given Babylonian names during the days of subjugation. So the origin of his name tells us nothing of his race or homeland. The term *Horonite* could mean Sanballat came from Beth-horon in Ephraim, or from Horonaim in Moab. He also could be named for the Canaanite god Horon (in fact, *Beth-horon means* "house of Horon"). Perhaps by calling Sanballat "the Horonite," Nehemiah was emphasizing that Sanballat was a worshiper of a pagan God.

Tobiah is called "the Ammonite official." Some have thought Tobiah is Sanballat's servant, but he probably is a servant to the king. In other words, he is a public official. Tobiah, then, was governor of Ammon by appointment of Artaxerxes.

❏ *Nehemiah 2:11-16.* Nehemiah arises in the night and makes an inspection of the city walls. He takes a few men with him, but no one else is aware of what he is doing. He has not yet told anyone that he plans to rebuild the walls.

The phrase *during the night* or *by night* occurs three times in these verses, emphasizing the secret nature of the inspection. The few men who accompany him undoubtedly are servants, since only Nehemiah rides a donkey (verse 12).

We are not sure of the exact location of the Valley Gate, but it was somewhere on the western wall. The Jackal Well is not mentioned anywhere else in the Bible. But it, too, must be on the western wall, since the next stop he makes, the Dung Gate, is on the southwestern wall, about a thousand cubits from the Valley Gate (3:13). The Dung Gate was used as the exit from the city to the Valley of Hinnom where all the refuse was taken for burning.

Next Nehemiah stops at the Fountain Gate. He now has reached the southeastern section of the wall. The fountain this gate led to may have been the Gihon Spring, but probably was Enrogel, the spring in the Kidron Valley close to where it is joined by the Valley of Hinnom. The King's Pool is undoubtedly the Pool of Siloam mentioned in 3:15. It was formed by shunting some of the waters form the Gihon Spring.

Nehemiah now has gone as far as he can and so he turns back. He re-enters the city through the same gate he had left from, the Valley Gate. Some have interpreted that to mean that

Nehemiah had encircled the entire city, but Nehemiah himself tells us that he turned back. Apparently the path between the city wall and the drop-off into the valley below had become too narrow for his donkey.

❑ *Nehemiah 2:17-20.* Nehemiah is now ready to tell his fellow Jews why he has come to Jerusalem—he wants to build the wall. He goes on to tell them what the king had said to him, and that the hand of God has been upon him throughout the whole episode. The people respond with enthusiasm.

But Sanballat and Tobiah appear on the scene again, and this time Geshem the Arab is with them. They want to know if Nehemiah is rebelling against the king.

Geshem must be the governor of the Arabian district. The way the question of the three governors is worded indicates that Nehemiah and his men are already at work. Their second question, ("Are you rebelling against the king?") is somewhat confusing in light of the fact that Nehemiah had shown them his letter from King Artaxerxes earlier (verse 9). Either the governors of verse 9 do not include these three, or the letter from Artaxerxes provides Nehemiah with safe passage, but does not mention that he is to rebuild the city. Perhaps Sanballat, Tobiah, and Geshem just want to intimidate Nehemiah even through they know Nehemiah has the king's approval.

Nehemiah's reply does not answer the questions they asked. His words, " The God of heaven will give us success" seem to be in response to the derision in verse 19 rather than the questions put to him. Their question about rebelling against the king goes unanswered, unless we assume the words *we his servants,* mean "we are Artaxerxes's servants." The context seems to indicate clearly, however, that they are God's servants.

Nehemiah manages to get in a few jibes himself. To "have no share in Jerusalem" means they do not own any of the land. To have no "claim or historic right in Jerusalem" is to have nothing there by which the people will remember them. Nehemiah is saying, therefore, you have no business here because you do not own any property here. Your authority stops at the district line, and once we get this wall built, even the memory of you will fade from existence!

DIMENSION THREE:
WHAT DOES THE BIBLE MEAN TO ME?

Nehemiah 1:4—Mourning for Jerusalem

When Nehemiah heard of the great trouble that the people of Jerusalem were in, he wept and mourned for days. Four and a half centuries later, Jesus contemplated the spiritual poverty of his people, and cried out, "O Jerusalem, Jerusalem, you who kill the prophets and stone those sent to you, how often I have longed to gather your children together, as a hen gathers her chicks under her wings, but you were not willing" (Matthew 23:37; Luke 13:34). Both men were deeply moved by the plight of their people. What does it take to move us to such cries of anguish? What is the nature of our spiritual poverty?

Nehemiah 2:4—Praying at Critical Moments

Nehemiah knows his well-being, perhaps even his life, is on the line when he tells Artaxerxes why he is sad. In the split moment between the time that Artaxerxes asks the question and the time that Nehemiah answers it, Nehemiah prayed to the God of heaven. Are such crisis prayers legitimate? Are such prayers a sign of a religious person? Or should we not use prayer as a way to receive divine aid in critical moments? When have you used crisis prayers?

Nehemiah 2:10-20—The Faith to See It Through

Sanballat and Tobiah were displeased that Nehemiah had come to help the people of Israel, and they let Nehemiah know it (2:10). In spite of that, Nehemiah challenges his people to build the wall of Jerusalem. Again Sanballat and Tobiah express their displeasure, this time joined by Geshem. They derided Nehemiah and his workers, despised them, and tried to scare them out of building the wall. But Nehemiah and his men still continued to work, saying "The God of heaven will give us success" (2:20). That not only takes determination; that takes faith.

NEHEMIAH THE CUPBEARER

How easily discouraged are we when things go wrong, when someone in authority tries to keep us from doing what we believe God would have us do, and when we are derided and despised and threatened? How strong is our faith? How does our faith help us in these situations?

So we rebuilt the wall till all of it
reached half its height (4:6).

— 6 —
Restoring the Wall
Nehemiah 3–5

DIMENSION ONE:
WHAT DOES THE BIBLE SAY?

Answer these questions by reading Nehemiah 3

1. Who is the high priest in Nehemiah's day? (3:1)

2. Does the high priest help rebuild the wall? (3:1)

3. What are some of the types of groups doing repair work? (3:2, 3, 12, 17)

4. What is different about those from the household of Shallum who work on the wall? (3:12)

Answer these questions by reading Nehemiah 4

5. How does Sanballat feel about the wall being rebuilt? (4:1)

6. What does Tobiah say? (4:3)

7. For what does Nehemiah pray? (4:4-5)

8. What groups plot to fight against the Jews? (4:7-8)

9. What do the Jews do then? (4:9)

10. What does Nehemiah tell the people? (4:14)

11. What precautions does Nehemiah have the people take? (4:16-18)

Answer these questions by reading Nehemiah 5

12. What three complaints do the people have? (5:1-4)

13. How does Nehemiah rectify the situation? (5:11-12)

14. How long is Nehemiah governor of Judah? (5:14)

15. How is Nehemiah different from the former governors of Judah? (5:14-15)

16. What prayer does Nehemiah pray as he remembers his years as governor? (5:19)

DIMENSION TWO: WHAT DOES THE BIBLE MEAN?

❏ *Nehemiah 3:1-32.* Nehemiah divides the work into approximately forty-four sections and assigns various workers to each section. Some workers work on more than one section.

We are told first where the high priest and other priests worked, namely at the Sheep Gate. They are responsible for the wall as far as the Tower of the Hundred and as far as the Tower of Hananal. Then we are told who worked next to them. The work is then described all the way around the wall (in a counterclockwise direction). In almost every case we are told who did the work, how much of the wall he (or the group) was responsible for, and who continued the work from there. By the time we get to verse 32, we are back to the Sheep Gate.

The Book of Nehemiah contains the best description of the Jerusalem wall in the Bible. The book mentions ten gates. Six of these gates are mentioned nowhere else in the Bible. In addition we are told of four towers, of the Broad Wall, the Pool of Siloam, the artificial pool, the angle, the tombs of David, and other places we have little information about.

RESTORING THE WALL   **45**

The Sheep Gate was located on the north wall close to where the northern and eastern walls joined. The sacrificial animals were brought through the gate into the city. It was no doubt for this reason that Eliashib and the priests worked there.

The Fish Gate is on the northern part of the wall close to the western corner. The marketplaces where the fishermen brought their fish to sell are located hear here. The fishermen entered and left the city through this gate.

The Jeshanah (or Old) Gate is mentioned only in the Book of Nehemiah (3:6; 12:39). All we know for sure is that it was located between the Fish Gate and the Broad Wall.

The Valley Gate, mentioned last session, is on the western wall, opening to the Valley of Hinnom (but not the section of Hinnom used as the garbage dump).

The Dung Gate is on the southwestern portion of the wall and is the gate used when carrying the refuse to the Valley of Hinnom for burning.

The Fountain Gate is on the eastern side of the wall close to the southern end. We are not sure which spring this fountain received its water from, but Enrogel would seem to be the best guess.

The Water Gate is on the eastern wall, farther north, and leads to the Gihon Spring.

The Horse Gate opens into the palace area and is called "the place where the horses enter the palace grounds" (2 Kings 11:16).

We do not know whether the East Gate is a separate gate or is to be identified with the Water Gate on the east. Another possibility is that the East Gate is an inner gate rather than one on the outer wall. See Ezekiel 46:1-8, for example, where Ezekiel sees a "gate of the inner court facing east."

The Inspection Gate is probably the gate before which the troops assembled when preparing for maneuvers or an attack. After the Inspection Gate and the upper chamber of the corner, there remains but little for the goldsmiths and the merchants to repair before they come again to the Sheep Gate.

❏ *Nehemiah 4:1-5.* When Sanballat hears that Nehemiah and his cohorts are building the wall, he is enraged. He wants to know what "those feeble Jews" are doing. Tobiah, with perhaps more of a sense of humor than Sanballat, said, in effect, What do we care if they are building a wall? Are they skilled workers? Of course not! Even a fox could break down their stone wall.

Nehemiah recognizes that Sanballat's anger might erupt into an actual assault on the Jewish people. It infuriates him that Sanballat is so intent on stopping the Lord's work. He prays for God to take vengeance on Sanballat and Tobiah.

❑ *Nehemiah 4:6-23.* The anger of Sanballat and the ridicule of Tobiah do not stop the Jews from working. In fact, they work harder. So the people of Judah complete the wall all around the city from the ground to half its height.

This further progress on the wall causes Sanballat and his allies to be very angry. They plot together with others of Judah's neighbors. Ridicule, derision, and intimidation obviously have not worked. They now determine to take sterner measures. Once again Nehemiah turns to God in prayer. This time, however, he also posts a guard as protection.

Then we are told that the people of Judah have heard a rumor that their enemies plan a sneak attack. The Jews who live outside the city, and by the enemies, confirm this rumor. So Nehemiah stations people with swords, spears, and bows. And he challenges the people not to be afraid of them, to remember the Lord, and to fight!

After that, half the people work on construction and half hold the weapons of war. Each worker works with one hand, and holds a weapon with the other. And each builder has on a sword while working. In this way Nehemiah's men are able to continue building the wall, but also are ready in case of attack. The working hours are extended, so that each person works from dawn until night. The trumpeter stands ready to sound the trumpet in case of attack, and the workmen sleep with their clothes on and weapons in hand.

❑ *Nehemiah 5:1-13.* Our attention is now shifted to some internal problems the people are facing. The poor complain about their Jewish brothers who are in positions of authority. They complain that they do not have enough grain to eat; that they have had to mortgage their fields, vineyards, and houses to buy food; and that they have had to borrow money to pay the king's tax. As a result of these hardships, their sons and daughters are forced to be slaves.

When Nehemiah hears of the plight of the poor, he calls a great assembly, and accuses the nobles and officials of charging interest. Then he says something that reveals to us a policy of his administration that we would not have known about otherwise. Nehemiah says, "We have bought back our Jewish brothers who were sold to the Gentiles." According to the law, Jewish people who became enslaved to other Jewish people were to be set free at the Year of Jubilee (Leviticus 25:39-41). Jewish people who became enslaved to foreigners, however, did not enjoy this privilege. They could be bought back, but they were not just voluntarily released (Leviticus 25:47-49). It is this practice to which Nehemiah refers. He says he has been buying Jews who have been sold to other nations. But the nobles are selling their brethren so that they can be sold back to the Jews. What an indictment!

What seems to have been happening is this. The poorer Jewish people did not have enough money for food, so they had to mortgage their property, and even their children, to buy grain from the nobles. Then, the nobles sold these children to the men of the surrounding nations. And Nehemiah discovers that some of the Jews he has been redeeming from slavery are the very ones who have been sold by the rich nobles. No wonder when he brings these charges against them, they are silent!

Then Nehemiah confesses he has been lending money and grain at interest, too. So, he says, "Let the exacting of usury stop!" Then, not waiting for the jubilee year, he wants to return their fields, their vineyards, their olive orchards, and their houses.

The nobles agree to Nehemiah's demands. But to be sure, Nehemiah calls in the priests and has the nobles and officials take an oath. To dramatize what he is about to say, Nehemiah shakes out his lap, the part of an outer garment that was used for a pocket. The people are now satisfied.

❑ *Nehemiah 5:14-19.* Nehemiah next tells us what a good governor he had been during his twelve years in that office. He lists his many good deeds. Then, in characteristic fashion,

Nehemiah prays: "Remember me with favor," he asks of God, "for all I have done for these people."

DIMENSION THREE:
WHAT DOES THE BIBLE MEAN TO ME?

Nehemiah 4:4-5—For What Should We Pray?

This prayer of Nehemiah has been a source of embarrassment to many. What place does a prayer like this have on the lips of one of the heroes of the Bible? Basically, what he is praying is, Let the worst you can imagine be done to them, O God! Then he adds, "Do not cover up their guilt." That is, keep it ever before you to remind you to do evil to them.

We can understand Nehemiah's bitterness. Sanballat and Tobiah had sought to frustrate his work at every turn. Sanballat had referred to the Jews as "those feeble Jews," and Tobiah had tried to make them a laughingstock with his remark about the fox running across the wall and knocking it over. But in spite of our sympathy for Nehemiah, we also know his prayer is a long way from Jesus' command to "love your enemies and pray for those who persecute you" (Matthew 5:44).

How would a Christian respond to a prayer like this? Do you think Nehemiah was justified in praying this prayer? Why or why not? When is a prayer for the hurt of another ever justified?

Nehemiah 5:7—Love Your Neighbor

Nehemiah's concern here is not that the Jewish nobles are exacting interest, but rather that they are exacting interest from their fellow Jews. The question that raises for us is, Is it worse to "do in" one of our own than it is to do the same thing to someone else? Are crimes committed against one's own family or ethnic group worse than the same crimes committed against someone else? Why or why not?

Nehemiah 5:12—Taking Oaths

When Nehemiah wanted to make the promise of the nobles binding, he had them take an oath in the presence of the priests. This was roughly the equivalent of the modern practice of swearing on a Bible. How does swearing on a Bible affect what we say? Does such an oath become more binding on us? Jesus said, "Do not swear at all . . . . Simply let your 'Yes' be 'Yes,' and your 'No,' 'No'; anything beyond this comes from the evil one" (Matthew 5:33-37). Why do we think it necessary to make a person swear that he or she is telling the truth?

*The whole company
numbered 42,360 (7:66).*

— 7 —
The Census
Nehemiah 6–7

DIMENSION ONE:
WHAT DOES THE BIBLE SAY?

Answer these questions by reading Nehemiah 6

1. What do Sanballat and Geshem do when they hear Nehemiah is completing the wall? (6:1-2)

2. Why does Nehemiah refuse to go? (6:2-3)

3. Of what does Sanballat accuse Nehemiah? (6:5-7)

4. What does Sanballat threaten to do? (6:7)

5. Why does Sanballat send this letter? (6:9)

6. How does Nehemiah reply to Sanballat? (6:8)

7. What does Shemaiah tell Nehemiah to do? (6:10)

8. Why doesn't Nehemiah follow Shemaiah's suggestion? (6:11-13)

9. What prayer does Nehemiah then pray? (6:14)

10. How long does it take to complete the wall? (6:15)

11. What do the enemies of Judah do when the wall is finished? (6:16)

12. Why are some persons in Judah bound by oath to Tobiah? (6:18)

Answer these questions by reading Nehemiah 7

13. Who does Nehemiah put in charge of Jerusalem? (7:2)

14. How does Nehemiah protect Jerusalem? (7:3)

15. Why does Nehemiah decide to take a census of the people? (7:4-5)

16. How many people are in the whole assembly? (7:66)

DIMENSION TWO:
WHAT DOES THE BIBLE MEAN?

❏ *Nehemiah 6:1-9.* Sanballat, Tobiah, and Geshem are no longer in the vicinity of Jerusalem, but they still are determined to keep Nehemiah from finishing the wall. When they hear that the wall is finished except for the doors, they send Nehemiah a message. They want to meet with him in one of the villages on the plain of Ono. Apparently they intend for this message to have the ring of reconciliation about it. But Nehemiah is shrewd enough to recognize that they intend to harm him. He therefore refuses their request by saying that he is doing important work and cannot leave. Four times they send him the same message; four times he gives them the same reply. Nehemiah will not give in.

Finally Sanballat sends a different message. Sanballat claims that it has been reported that Nehemiah and the Jews intend to rebel against Artaxerxes, and "therefore you are building the wall." Sanballat also accuses Nehemiah of wanting to become king of Judah, and having prophets to proclaim him king. These things, says Sanballat, will be reported to the king. So Nehemiah should come and talk to him about it.

In the first four messages Sanballat sends to Nehemiah, he pretends to be reaching out in peace. Possibly this letter could be read in that same light. Sanballat could be pretending to write out of concern for Nehemiah. Then the meaning of the letter would be: There are a lot of rumors going around that you are rebuilding the Jerusalem wall so you can have yourself proclaimed as king of Judah. You know reports like that are bound to get back to Artaxerxes. Come, let us meet together to decide what we can do about it.

That would be the meaning if Sanballat were still feigning friendship. It is difficult to believe, however, that he would think Nehemiah naive enough to swallow that. It seems more likely that since his first four messages did not convince Nehemiah to meet with him, Sanballat is here reverting to his old tactics of fear and intimidation. Sanballat's letter was intended to be seen not as a friendly warning, but as a threat. Sanballat is saying that he will tell Artaxerxes that Nehemiah is planning a revolt. And Nehemiah knows what the consequences of that report would be!

The plain of Ono is a good fifteen miles from Jerusalem, and is in a district controlled by neither Judah nor Samaria. Sanballat could possibly use this as a good reason for them to meet there. However, Nehemiah knew that it would be all too easy for Sanballat to lay a trap to have him killed there. Sanballat would then have it appear that outside marauders had attacked them. Nehemiah therefore sends a message back to Sanballat telling him that he has made these things up in his own mind. Then, once again, Nehemiah goes to God in prayer.

❏ *Nehemiah 6:10-14.* Tobiah and Sanballat now try a new ploy. They hire Shemaiah to try to get Nehemiah to lock himself in the Temple with Shemaiah. Shemaiah tells Nehemiah that someone is going to kill him.

We are not sure just who this Shemaiah was. His name is not an uncommon one, but nowhere else do we find a Shemaiah the son of Delaiah. Some commentators believe Shemaiah was a false prophet. However, it is more likely that he was a priest, since lay persons were not allowed in the Temple where the altar was. Neither Shemaiah nor Nehemiah seem to think it improper for him to go there.

Shemaiah proposes to Nehemiah that they go to the house of God, within the Temple, and hide there. Had he stopped with "the house of God," his suggestion would have been proper, for that term refers to the whole Temple complex. But when he added, "inside the temple," he was talking about an area where only priests were admitted. Nehemiah therefore refuses to go. "Should one like me," he asks, "go into the temple to save his life?" Only priests can enter there! (Numbers 18:7).

Nehemiah also had another reason for refusing Shemaiah's suggestion. Nehemiah does not think the governor of Judah should run and hide in fear. No, he tells Shemaiah, he will not go hide in the Temple.

Nehemiah's third reason for refusing to go he shares only with his readers, not with Shemaiah. He understood that God had not sent Shemaiah, but that Tobiah and Sanballat had hired him. Nehemiah was not taken in by Shemaiah's pretense of concern for his safety. He knew Tobiah and Sanballat wanted him to sin so they could ruin his reputation.

Nehemiah once again prays, and once again his prayer is for his enemies to be hurt (4:4-5).

❑ *Nehemiah 6:15-19.* The wall is finally finished. The story of its building has taken all or parts of Chapters 2, 3, 4, and 6. Yet it was completed in only fifty-two days! This is a remarkable feat under even the best of circumstances. Nehemiah's enemies and all the neighboring nations recognize the achievement is extraordinary, and are afraid.

Tobiah, however, does not give up in his attempt to discredit Nehemiah in the eyes of the people. He carries on an extensive correspondence with some of the nobles of Judah. These persons try to toot Tobiah's horn at the expense of Nehemiah, and they report what Nehemiah says to Tobiah. Tobiah apparently also sends letters to Nehemiah to frighten him.

❑ *Nehemiah 7:1-5.* After the completion of the city walls, and the setting up of the gatekeepers, the singers, and the Levites, Nehemiah appoints Hanani and Hananiah to be in charge of Jerusalem. The interference of Sanballat and Tobiah subsides, but Nehemiah knows that precautions must still be taken. He orders that the gates not be opened each day until the sun is hot. That would keep the enemy from coming in and overpowering the city while most of the people were still asleep. Nor are the guards to be released from their duties until the gates are secured at night.

Then God puts it into Nehemiah's mind to take a census. The task he has come to Jerusalem for is to rebuild it (2:5). The first part of that task is now complete; the wall is rebuilt. But there is more to a city than its walls. As yet there are only a few people in Jerusalem. Nehemiah needs to know who these people are, and how many there are. So he initiates a census. In the process, he discovers "the genealogical record of those who had been the first to return."

❏ *Nehemiah 7:6-73.* The names listed here are almost identical to those listed in Ezra 2:1-70.

DIMENSION THREE:
WHAT DOES THE BIBLE MEAN TO ME?

Nehemiah 6:3—When Is a Lie not a Lie?

When Sanballat and Tobiah sent word to Nehemiah for him to meet them in the plain of Ono, Nehemiah sent back the word, "I am carrying on a great project and cannot go down. Why should the work stop while I leave it and go down to you?" No equivocation there! Nehemiah makes it plain he has no intentions of meeting with his two adversaries.

In the Septuagint version (a Greek translation made in the third century B.C.) what Nehemiah says is this: "I am doing a great work and I cannot come down lest the work stop. When I have finished, I will come down to you." If this is really what Nehemiah said, there seems to be a bit of deception in his words. Nehemiah has already said he perceived that "they were scheming to harm me" (verse 2). He would have no intention, then, of meeting with Sanballat and Tobiah. His words would seem to be a delaying technique, a way of gaining some time to work on the walls.

Now, let us assume for the moment that the Septuagint reading is the true one. The question we must ask is, Can we legitimately deceive an evil person to keep that person from hindering a good work? Or, are we simply adding to the amount of evil in the world if we deceive someone, even if it is for a good cause? When does the good end we wish to achieve make it all right to use an evil method to achieve that end? And who has the responsibility for making that decision?

Nehemiah 7:2—Leadership Qualities

When Nehemiah needed someone to be in charge of Jerusalem, he selected persons who were people "of integrity and feared God more than most men do." What qualities do we look for in our leaders? How important is it that our mayor, our governor, our senators, or our president be faithful and God-fearing? Are these qualities that we look for when we cast our ballot? How do such qualities in our leaders affect our daily lives?

And all the people listened attentively
to the Book of the Law (8:3).

— 8 —
The Book of the Law
Nehemiah 8–10

DIMENSION ONE:
WHAT DOES THE BIBLE SAY?

Answer these questions by reading Nehemiah 8

1. Where do the people gather? (8:1)

2. What does Ezra read to the people? (8:1, 3)

3. How do Jeshua and the others help the people? (8:7)

4. What do the people do when they hear the word of the law? (8:9)

5. Why do the Levites calm the people? (8:11)

6. What do the people discover God has commanded them to do during the feast of the seventh month? (8:13-14)

7. What do the people do then? (8:15-16)

8. How long do the people keep the feast? (8:18)

Answer these questions by reading Nehemiah 9

9. What do the people do on the twenty-fourth day of the month? (9:1-2)

10. In his prayer, what does Ezra say their forefathers did? (9:16)

11. How does Ezra say God responded to the disobedience of the forefathers? (9:17, 20)

12. How does Ezra say the people responded to these new acts of grace on God's part? (9:26)

13. What does Ezra say God did then? (9:27)

14. What does Ezra say God finally did? (9:30)

15. Does Ezra believe God has been just? (9:33)

16. What does Ezra say is the plight of the Israelites today? (9:36-37)

17. What do the people do now, and what do the leaders, Levites, and priests do? (9:38)

Answer these questions by reading Nehemiah 10

18. What do the people pledge to do? (10:29)

19. What laws do the people pledge to keep? (10:30-31)

20. How do the people pledge to support the work of the Temple? (10:32-37)

21. Where are these offerings to be taken and kept? (10:38-39)

DIMENSION TWO:
WHAT DOES THE BIBLE MEAN?

Where does Chapter 8 begin? Sounds like a silly question, doesn't it? But notice in the New International Version that the paragraph division comes not with the first verse of Chapter 8, but with the last portion of the last verse of Chapter 7. The words, "When the seventh month came and the Israelites had settled in their towns," are not the conclusion to what has been said in Chapter 7. They are the introduction to what follows in Chapter 8. So, they belong in Chapter 8.

❑ *Nehemiah 8:1-8.* The people of Israel gather in the square in front of the Water Gate. Ezra brings the Book of the Law of Moses and reads from it as the people listen. He reads from early morning until midday and everyone listens attentively.

Ezra stands on a wooden pulpit as he reads, and is flanked by thirteen of his comrades. The people lift their hands and say "Amen! Amen!" as Ezra blesses the Lord. They bow their heads, and worship God with their faces to the ground. The Levites help the people to understand the law and translate it for them.

❑ *Nehemiah 8:2.* Assembly may be too formal a word to describe the gathering. Two manuscripts use the word *multitude,* and one says simply *people.* Usually only the men gathered for religious instruction but here both men and women gathered, as well as the children old enough to understand. That emphasizes the importance attached to this meeting.

❑ *Nehemiah 8:3.* Ezra is said to have read from the Book of the Law from early morning until midday. Therefore, the document must have been fairly long. In spite of the lengthy reading, the people were attentive the whole time. If the children became restless, no mention is made of it.

❑ *Nehemiah 8:4.* The Hebrew word translated as *a high wooden platform* actually means "tower." The people had "built [this platform] for the occasion." The word here translated *occasion,* however, more strictly means "word." The platform, then, might be an old one, built not for this purpose but as a speaker's platform. It stands in the square, and is used whenever a speaker is addressing a large crowd.

The names of the men standing with Ezra are given to us, but since no family names are given, we have no idea who these men might be. Perhaps the most we can say is that several important men of Israel stand with Ezra as he reads the law to the people. Their presence gives affirmation to Ezra's words.

❑ *Nehemiah 8:5.* As Ezra opens the book, all the people rise. This is a way to pay respect to and to honor the authority of the words about to be read. It may be that in this act we have the beginning of the custom of rising when the Scripture is read in church. Or this may be a liturgical custom already established.

❑ *Nehemiah 8:6.* The word *amen* here means "so be it" and is a way of adding emphasis to what is being said. Their hands are lifted with their palms up in the accepted posture for prayer in Ezra's day. Then the people bow their heads, and worship God with their faces to the ground. This is the accepted and practiced position of worship for Muslims today.

❑ *Nehemiah 8:8.* To say the Levites "read from the Book of the Law of God, making it clear" is to say that they read it with interpretation so that it was clearly understood. Apparently Ezra reads from the Hebrew, and the Levites translate what Ezra reads into Aramaic, the tongue of the people.

❑ *Nehemiah 8:9-12.* Apparently the people are conscience-stricken, for they know that neither they nor their ancestors had kept the law. They know, too—perhaps they even hear Ezra read to them—how God will punish a wayward and unrepentant people (Leviticus 26:14-39).

But the Levites hush the people, telling them not to mourn, but rather to rejoice, because this day is holy.

❑ *Nehemiah 8:10.* Not only are the people to eat and drink, they are also to "send some to those who have nothing prepared," that is, the poor.

❑ *Nehemiah 8:13-18.* The next day the "heads of all the families," the priests, and the Levites study the words of the law again. As they do so, they discover the laws concerning the feast of the seventh month (Deuteronomy 16:13-15; Leviticus 23:33-43). The leaders then have the people go out and gather branches to make booths. They keep the feast for seven days, while Ezra reads from the Book of the Law.

62   EZRA, NEHEMIAH, AND ESTHER

❑ *Nehemiah 9:1-5.* The festivities and merriment are now over. The people gather once again, but this time to fast and mourn. They are to separate themselves from all foreigners and to confess their sins. Wearing a sackcloth and putting dirt on their heads is a sign of anguish or mourning.

❑ *Nehemiah 9:6-37.* This long, penitential prayer is attributed to Ezra, but the Hebrew text does not name Ezra. The prayer is preceded by a doxology, an ascription of praise to God (verse 5). The prayer itself is basically a review of Israel's history, designed to show God's unending grace toward Israel, even during her times of apostasy. The prayer has much in common with Psalms 78; 105; and 106. See also Acts 7.

❑ *Nehemiah 9:6.* The term *highest heavens* is not frequent in the Old Testament, but it does occur (Deuteronomy 10:14). The Jewish idea of a multiplicity of heavens carries over into the New Testament as well (2 Corinthians 12:2; Ephesians 4:10). The highest heavens is heaven *par excellence.* The starry host is a group of God's attendants, sometimes personified (1 Kings 22:19) and sometimes thought of as the sun, moon, and stars (Deuteronomy 4:19).

❑ *Nehemiah 9:9.* This event is recorded in Exodus 14:9-10.

❑ *Nehemiah 9:14-15.* "Through your servant Moses" is literally, by the hand of Moses.

❑ *Nehemiah 9:16.* The author now turns his attention to the people. God had been gracious to them; how did they respond? They responded by acting *arrogant and stiff-necked.* The Hebrew word here translated *arrogant and stiff-necked* is the same word that is translated *arrogantly* in verse 10. That is to say, their ancestors acted just like the pharaoh and his people!

❑ *Nehemiah 9:22.* The author recognized that it was God who enabled their ancestors to take kingdoms and peoples, beginning with the land of Sihon, king of Heshbon, and the land of Og, king of Bashan.

❑ *Nehemiah 9:23.* God fulfills the promise to Abraham that his seed shall be "as the stars in the sky" (Genesis 15:5; 22:17; 26:4).

❑ *Nehemiah 9:25-26.* The Israelites move in and take over the land of the Canaanites, including their houses and their vineyards. They eat and are filled. Indeed, they become well-filled because of God's generosity. But having an overabundance in

THE BOOK OF THE LAW **63**

the Old Testament often has the meaning of *unresponsiveness*, that is, unresponsive to God (Isaiah 6:10). The people rebel against God, kill the prophets, and commit great blasphemies. ❏ *Nehemiah 9:27-31.* To bring them to their senses, God gives the Israelites into the hand of their enemy. The people repent and cry for help. God hears their cry and sends them a savior. But as soon as things are going well again, the people forget God and turn again to their evil.

❏ *Nehemiah 9:32-37.* The author now turns his thoughts to his own day. He pleads to God not to continue to punish them for the sins of their ancestors. He says the people are slaves and are in great distress.

❏ *Nehemiah 9:38—10:27.* Then follow the names of those who make a covenant. The contents of the covenant are given later. The names are listed by categories, as is usual. First the names of Nehemiah and Zedekiah appear. We do not know who Zedekiah is. But he must be an important figure, or he would not be named so early in the list. Some believe he is to be identified with Zadok (ZAD-dock), Nehemiah's scribe (13:13), but we know of no other instance where *Zadok* is used as an abbreviation of Zedekiah. Priest are named next, verses 2-8; then the Levites, verses 9-13; and finally the "leaders of the people" (the lay heads of families), verses 14-27.

❏ *Nehemiah 10:28-39.* The things that the people promise to do are 1) not to marry the peoples of the lands, 2) not to buy on the sabbath or on a holy day, 3) not to reap the crops of the seventh year or accept payment for debts, 4) to pay a Temple tax, 5) to gather wood for the altar, 6) to bring the first fruits to the Temple, 7) and to bring the Levites the tithes.

❏ *Nehemiah 10:30.* The main concern in forbidding marriage with foreign people is to keep the Israelite region pure. The command not to marry foreign women is given in Deuteronomy 7:1-3. The reason is given in Exodus 34:12-16.

❏ *Nehemiah 10:31.* The practices described in Nehemiah 13:15-22 were making the sabbath like any other day. The people pledge, therefore, not to buy from the people of the land on the sabbath or on a holy day. They go even further. Talk of the seventh day brings to mind the seventh year, so they pledge that "every seventh year we will forgo working the land and will cancel all debts," as commanded in Exodus 23:10-11, Leviticus 25:2-7, and Deuteronomy 15:1-11.

❏ *Nehemiah 10:37.* "A tithes of our crops" were to be given to God (Leviticus 27:30). Notice that the Levites collect the tithes. There is no law providing for that, but evidently that seemed to be the best way of collecting the tithes.

DIMENSION THREE:
WHAT DOES THE BIBLE MEAN TO ME?

Nehemiah 8:13-18
How Binding on Us Are the Bible's Commands?

When the Israelite people discovered that the law said they should live in booths during the feast of the seventh month, they cut down trees and made booths. They were determined to do as the law said.

That command is still in the Bible (Leviticus 23:42), but we feel no obligation to observe it. We think of ourselves as being "Bible-believing Christians," yet here is a law clearly stated in the Bible, and we make no attempt to follow it. Why? When may we ignore some of the commands of the Bible? If we ignore some of the commands of the Bible, is it then okay to ignore all of them? And if not, how do we decide which we must obey and which we can safely ignore?

Nehemiah 9:16—Responding to God's Grace

God acted graciously toward the people, but they responded by acting arrogant and stiff-necked! At what times in the history of the church has God acted graciously toward the people, and they, the church, acted arrogant and stiff-necked in return? At what times in your own life have you done the same thing?

Nehemiah 9:29—Seek Ye the Lord!

This verse is very law oriented. Whereas 9:26 says the people were warned in order to get them to turn back to God, this verse says they were warned in order to get them to turn back to God's *law*. And whereas in Amos 5:4 God says, "Seek me and live," this verse says that by the observance of God's ordinances, a person shall live.

The distinction may seem slight, but the consequences are great. It is possible to come back to God's law for all the wrong reasons—the fear of punishment, or the embarrassment of getting caught. But when we come back to God, we come only out of love. A self-seeking return to God's law may prove to be short lives; a return to God is more likely to be permanent. A return to God's ordinances does not necessarily mean a return to God, but a return to God most assuredly means a return to God's law.

Jesus called us to do both. Seek first, he said, God's kingdom and God's righteousness (Matthew 6:33). Can you see this distinction in your own life between a return to God and a return to God's law? When have you returned to God's law for the wrong reason? When have you returned to God?

Nehemiah 9:31—What Is God Like?

We often hear that the God of the Old Testament is a God of wrath, and the God of the New Testament is a God of love. Do you believe that statement to be true or false? or somewhere in between true and false? Why do you think so? How does Nehemiah 9:31 confirm or deny your belief?

*So I purified the priests and the
Levites of everything foreign (13:30).*

9
Nehemiah's Reforms
Nehemiah 11–13

DIMENSION ONE:
WHAT DOES THE BIBLE SAY?

Answer these questions by reading Nehemiah 11

1. How do the people decide who will live in Jerusalem?
(11:1)

2. How are the people who live in Jerusalem listed? (11:4, 7,
10, 15, 19, 21)

3. In what two territories are the villages occupied by Jews
located? (11:25, 31)

Answer these questions by reading Nehemiah 12

4. Who were the high priests from the days of the return
from Babylon to this time? (12:10-11)

5. What celebration now takes place? (12:27)

6. What do the priests and Levites do before the dedication? (12:30)

7. How many large choirs does Nehemiah appoint to go in procession? (12:31)

8. In which directions do the two choirs go? (12:31, 38)

9. Where do the two choirs meet? (12:40)

10. What takes place then? (12:43)

11. For what job does Nehemiah appoint men on that day? (12:44)

Answer these questions by reading Nehemiah 13

12. What do the people discover as they read from the Book of Moses? (13:1)

13. What do the people do then? (13:3)

14. What does Eliashib do for Tobiah? (13:4-5)

15. What does Nehemiah do when he discovers this? (13:8-9)

16. Why does Nehemiah appoint treasurers? (13:10-11, 13)

17. What does Nehemiah do when he sees men working and selling their wares on the sabbath? (13:15, 17, 19)

18. What command does Nehemiah give to the Levites? (13:22)

19. What does Nehemiah do to the Jews who had married women of Ashdod, Ammon, and Moab? (13:23-25)

20. What summary of his reforms does Nehemiah give? (13:30-31)

DIMENSION TWO:
WHAT DOES THE BIBLE MEAN?

❏ *Nehemiah 11:1-2.* The wall of Jerusalem is restored and the gates are secured. The city is ready for habitation and can offer security to those who live there. Some, therefore, go to live in Jerusalem willingly, but most do not. They are settled in the other towns, and are understandably reluctant to move. But since a city must have inhabitants to survive, a plan is devised whereby lots are cast, and one out of ten is selected to move to Jerusalem. Though the text does not say so, it seems reasonable to assume that the people move as family units. That is, one out of ten families moves rather than one out of ten persons.

Why is Jerusalem called "the holy city"? And why do we commonly call Palestine the Holy Land? Not, as some Christians imagine, because Jesus lived there, though that would be reason enough to do so. But Jerusalem is called "the holy city" even in the Old Testament (Isaiah 48:2; 52:1; Daniel 9:24). Why? The designation probably arises as an extension of the name *Holy of Holies,* that most sacred room of the Temple. If that room is holy, then so is the entire Temple, the city in which the Temple is located, and the nation.

❏ *Nehemiah 11:1-24.* This list follows the same format as the lists given in Ezra 2 and Nehemiah 7:6-72. That is, the lay leaders are listed first, then the priests, the Levites, and the lesser officials.

One would expect a longer list than this of the descendants of Judah (verses 3-6). Even recognizing that the list is incomplete, we still should expect more than two families to be listed. But we read only about the family of Athaiah and that of Maaseiah. The list of the sons of Benjamin (verses 7-9) also is unexpectedly short. The list of priests (verses 10-14) and the list of Levites (verses 15-18) are more the length we should expect, and they closely parallel the corresponding lists in 1 Chronicles 9:10-16.

❏ *Nehemiah 11:25-36.* Having listed the people who live in Jerusalem, the author now turns to the Jews in the outlying towns. Since the leaders of the people all lived in Jerusalem

(11:1), the names of the families are not listed, but rather the names of the towns where they live. First, seventeen towns are listed (verses 25-30). These correspond very closely to the towns listed as given to the people of Judah in Joshua 15. Then the author lists fifteen towns where the people of Benjamin lived (verses 31-36). Only three of these are found in the list of Benjamite towns given in Joshua 18. Some of the towns listed as Benjamite towns were given originally to Dan and Ephraim. They became Benjamite towns by a two-step process. First, some of Dan's territory went to Judah and some to Ephraim during the period of the judges. Then, after the fall of Northern Israel, the southern portions of Ephraim became the possessions of Benjamin.

❑ *Nehemiah 12:1-26.* When Zerubbabel and Jeshua first brought a group back to Jerusalem from their exile in Babylon, Jeshua became the first high priest of the post-exilic era. The priests and Levites who served with him are listed in verses 1-7 and verses 8-9, respectively.

Joiakim, the son of Jeshua, was the next high priest, but before listing the priests and Levites who served with him, our author gives us the succession of high priests down to, and including, Jaddua (verses 10-11). Then the priests during the time of Joiakim are listed (verses 12-21). We should expect a list of the Levites next, but instead we are told that the genealogical record during the days of Eliashib, Joiada, Johanan, and Jaddua (Jah-DOO-ah), was kept (verses 22-23). At least a part of this record was written in the Book of the Chronicles in our Old Testament. It is a book, now lost, in which the official records of the Temple were kept.

After this interruption, the author lists the Levites during the time of Joiakim (verses 24-26). Then, once again, we are fooled. We expect the author to list the priests and the Levites during the times of all the other high priests. But these are not listed. Either a part of this work has been lost, or else the author believed that the simple statement that these records were kept was sufficient.

❑ *Nehemiah 12:27-43.* We are hardly prepared for what comes next. We have been reading lists of priests and Levites all the way down to Jaddua during the days of Alexander the Great.

Now suddenly, without any kind of transition, the author says "at the dedication of the wall of Jerusalem"! The wall was completed a century earlier, and has not been mentioned in Nehemiah's book since Chapter 7. Surely something is out of place.

The place where verses 27-43 would fit best is immediately following 6:15. Moreover, 6:16 follows naturally after verses 27-43. Many believe, therefore, that these verses originally stood after 6:15. Certainly the dedication would have taken place shortly after, if not immediately after, the completion of the wall.

The Levites and the singers are gathered together in order to celebrate the dedication. Before the dedication begins, the priests and the Levites purify themselves, the people, the gates, and the wall.

To begin the dedication Nehemiah appoints two great companies that then march in procession. One goes to the right upon the wall, and the other goes to the left. The two groups meet near the Temple. The singers sing, the priests offer sacrifices, and everyone, even the women and children, rejoices.

❑ *Nehemiah 12:44-47.* The thought behind these verses is that the system of worship set up by David was exactly the way it should have been, and this perfect system has been in operation in the Temple from the time of Zerubbabel to the time of Nehemiah. The priests, Levites, singers, and gatekeepers all perform their duties according to the command of David. The people give daily portions of their crops for the singers and gatekeepers. The people also set apart crops and food for the priests. That is the way things should be, and that is the way things were, right up to the time of Nehemiah.

❑ *Nehemiah 13.* Nehemiah had spent twelve years in Jerusalem during his first term as governor (5:14). Then he returned to Persia. After some time, Nehemiah again asked the king that he be allowed to return to Jerusalem. Permission was granted, and it was during his second term as governor that Nehemiah put into effect the reforms mentioned in Chapter 13.

❑ *Nehemiah 13:1-3.* We remember Tobiah from the days when Nehemiah was overseeing the rebuilding of the city walls. He was one of three leaders in the movement to stop work on the wall. He also used to cause Nehemiah grief by sending letters to the nobles and his in-laws in the city (6:17-19). Apparently after Nehemiah was in firm control of the city, he was able to keep Tobiah from causing any more trouble. When Nehemiah returns to Persia, however, the way is left open for Tobiah to re-establish himself. Eliashib the priest prepares a large chamber for Tobiah and apparently he and his family just move in. This makes Nehemiah very angry, and upon his return to Jerusalem, he throws all of Tobiah's furniture out of the chamber. He also gives orders that the chambers be cleaned and he returns the vessels of the house of God.

❑ *Nehemiah 13:10-14.* We are told in 12:47 that "in the days of Zerubbabel and of Nehemiah, all Israel contributed the daily portions for the singers and gatekeepers." But Nehemiah does not find that to be true when he returns from Persia. The Levites had not been given their portion. The plight of the Levites is so bad that they have to farm in order to make a living. Nehemiah complains to the officials and puts the Levites in their stations. Then Nehemiah appoints treasurers over the storehouses who distribute the tithes to their brethren. Then he prays that God will remember him concerning this.

❑ *Nehemiah 13:15-22.* Nehemiah is appalled as he observes the breaking of the sabbath regulations in Jerusalem. Regulations are being broken by foreigners as well as Nehemiah's own people. Men from Tyre and others whose religion does not prohibit them from trading on the sabbath are making wine, bringing in grain and other wares, and selling them seven days a week. And the Jews, whose religion does prohibit buying and selling on the sabbath, are purchasing these items seven days a week.

Nehemiah tells them they are profaning the sabbath day. He also tells them their fathers acted this way and God punished this city. Yet they bring more wrath upon Israel by profaning the sabbath.

Nehemiah takes steps to correct the situation by ordering that the gates of Jerusalem will be shut the evening before the sabbath and the doors will not be opened until after the sabbath. Then, to make sure his order is carried out, Nehemiah set some of his servants over the gates. But the merchants still congregate outside Jerusalem and apparently still carry on their trade there. So Nehemiah warns them, "If you do this again, I will lay hands on you." Nehemiah then has the Levites come and guard the gate. He prays again, asking God to "remember me for this also."

❑ *Nehemiah 13:23-31.* The mixed marriages are the next problem for Nehemiah. Jewish men had married women of Ashdod, Ammon, and Moab, and such marriages could lead to only one thing, the pollution of the Jewish religion. Therefore Nehemiah "rebuked them and called curses down on them . . . beat some of the men and pulled out their hair." He then makes them take an oath promising not to intermarry with these people.

One offender, one of the sons of Joiada, the son of Eliashib the high priest, was also the son-in-law of Sanballat, Nehemiah's old enemy. Nehemiah says he chased this person from him. Then, characteristically, Nehemiah offers a prayer to God.

DIMENSION THREE:
WHAT DOES THE BIBLE MEAN TO ME?

Nehemiah 13:1-3—Christianity and Xenophobia

Xenophobia is the fear of or the hatred of foreigners. There is a great deal of xenophobia in our world and in our nation. The clear teaching of Jesus and of Christianity is that we are to love all persons (Matthew 5:43-44). How can we reconcile these two?

Some have used passages like Nehemiah 13:1-3 to justify their racial prejudice or their dislike of persons from other nations. Would this verse support such prejudice? Why or why not? Were the Ammonites and Moabites to be excluded because they were foreigners or for some other reason? For what reasons should persons be excluded from our churches today? Or should they never be excluded? Why?

Nehemiah 13:25—When Others Disappoint Us

How do we usually react when others disappoint us or do things that we think they should not do? How should we react? Notice the ways in which Ezra and Nehemiah reacted to the same situation. When Ezra heard that the people of Israel had not separated themselves from the people of the land, he expressed his grief and dismay by pulling hair from his head and beard. Nehemiah responded by pulling out hair, too, but from the heads of the offenders! (Ezra 9:1-5) Ezra identified with his people, and spoke of their iniquities in his prayer (Ezra 9:6). Nehemiah prayed, too, but he prayed for God to remember that these people "defiled the priestly office" (Nehemiah 13:29).

Which of these two ways of reacting to offenders is closer to the way you might react? Think of specific examples where you or someone you know reacted in a way similar to that of either Ezra or Nehemiah. How can we learn to react to our disappointments in appropriate ways?

*Now the king was attracted to Esther more than
to any of the other women (2:17).*

10

Esther Becomes Queen

Esther 1–3

The Book of Esther has the dubious distinction of being
the only book in the Bible in which God is not mentioned.
Search as we may, we cannot find God explicitly referred to
even once. Furthermore, neither prayer nor worship nor any
religious festival is mentioned. None of the great themes of
the Old Testament, such as the Exodus or the covenant, is
given even brief notice. And none of the great virtues of the
Bible, such as love, forgiveness, and mercy are mentioned in
the story of Esther.

Esther did not become a part of the Hebrew Bible until the
council of Jamnia in A.D. 90 (some sixty or more years after
the death of Jesus), and its inclusion in the canon was a matter
of controversy from the very first. Once its place in the Hebrew
Bible was secure, its inclusion in the Christian Bible was auto-
matic, since the entire Hebrew Bible became the Christian Old
Testament. But sensitive persons, both Jewish and Christian,
have wondered at its inclusion, and have been embarrassed by
the ethics it propounds.

The book is not devoid of all religious value, however,
though some have claimed that it is. A few veiled references to
religion appear, and in one place God is almost certainly
referred to. These places will be pointed out as we make our
way through the book.

DIMENSION ONE:
WHAT DOES THE BIBLE SAY?

Answer these questions by reading Esther 1

1. For whom does Xerxes give a banquet, and for how long? (1:1-4)

2. After this banquet is over, for whom does Xerxes give another banquet, and how long does it last? (1:5)

3. Why does Xerxes become angry with Queen Vashti? (1:10-12)

4. What does Memucan propose that Xerxes send to all the people in his kingdom? (1:19)

5. What edict does Xerxes actually send to all the people in his kingdom? (1:22)

Answer these questions by reading Esther 2

6. How does Xerxes decide to replace Vashti as queen? (2:2-4)

7. Who is selected to be queen? (2:15-17)

8. Why is Mordecai's name recorded in the book of the annals of the king? (2:19-23)

Answer these questions by reading Esther 3

9. Who does Xerxes promote to second in command in the kingdom? (3:1)

10. Who refuses to bow down to Haman, and for what reason? (3:2-4)

11. What does Haman want to do? (3:5-6)

12. What does Haman say in a letter he sends to the governors and nobles of every province? (3:12-13)

13. How do the people react to Haman's letter? (3:15)

DIMENSION TWO:
WHAT DOES THE BIBLE MEAN?

❑ *Esther 1:1-22.* King Xerxes, who is also known by the Hebrew form of his name, Ahasuerus, gives a huge banquet that lasts for a hundred and eighty days. This banquet is held for all his princes and servants, the army chiefs, and the nobles and governors of the provinces. Immediately following, the king gives another banquet, this time for all the men in Susa, the capital. At the same time Vashti, the queen, gives a banquet for all the women. These banquets last seven days.

On the seventh day of the banquet, when the king is "in high spirits with wine," he orders the seven eunuchs who serve his queen to bring Queen Vashti before the king with her royal crown, so he can show everyone how beautiful she is. Vashti refuses, thereby embarrassing and infuriating the king.

Xerxes asks his wise men what should be done to Vashti according to the law. One of the men, Memucan, tells the king that Queen Vashti has done wrong, not only to the king, but to all the princes and people in the provinces as well. All women will hear about what Vashti has done and they will look at their husbands with contempt. In other words, Xerxes will be doing all men a favor if he punishes Vashti severely, and lets that punishment be known throughout the empire. Therefore, suggests Memucan, "let him issue a royal decree . . . that Vashti is never again to enter the presence of King Xerxes." Also, he suggests that the king give her royal position to another woman. Xerxes likes Memucan's suggestion, and sends letters to the provinces saying that every man is to be the lord of his own house.

❑ *Esther 2:1-18.* After his anger has subsided, the king remembers Vashti. Apparently we are to understand that he remembers her with fondness, though the meaning may be that the memory of her rekindled his anger. At any rate, Xerxes appoints officers in all the provinces of his kingdom to seek out all the beautiful young virgins and take them to the harem in Susa. He will then select the one who will become the queen. The women are first given ointments so they can make themselves even more beautiful.

Now for the first time the main characters are introduced. Mordecai was a Benjamite, just as King Saul of long ago had been (1 Samuel 9:1-2). Mordecai had brought up Hadassah, that is, Esther. Beautiful and lovely Esther is taken with all the other young virgins to Susa and put in the custody of Hegai, the king's eunuch in charge of the women.

Esther becomes a favorite of Hegai, who goes out of his way to provide her with the best of everything. She does not reveal the fact that she is a Jew because Mordecai told her not to. Mordecai does not forget his beautiful cousin, but walks in front of the court of the harem every day to learn how Esther is doing.

After the women have undergone a year's beautification program, they are each sent in to King Xerxes. As each goes in to see the king, she is allowed to take whatever she wishes with her. Each maiden goes in to see the king in the evening, and in the morning she is taken to the second harem. These women then become concubines of the king.

Apparently most of the virgins took expensive clothing or jewels from the harem with them, either as a way of impressing the king, or because they were allowed to keep what they took. But when Esther goes to the king, she takes nothing except what Hegai the king's eunuch suggests. Esther trusts Hegai to advise her on the king's taste. When Xerxes sees Esther, the search is over. He is attracted to Esther more than to all the other women. He puts the royal crown on her head and makes her queen instead of Vashti. The king then gives a great banquet to celebrate.

❏ *Esther 2:19-23.* Some time later (we are not told how much later), Mordecai becomes aware of the fact that Bigthana and Teresh, two of the king's eunuchs are plotting to assassinate the king. Mordecai tells Queen Esther, and Esther tells the king. An investigation is held, and it is found that what Mordecai has said is true. Bigthana and Teresh, therefore, are both "hanged on a gallows." The Hebrew text says they were *hanged on the wood.* Some have wondered whether the meaning might not be *impalement* rather than *hanging.* Others have thought that a form of crucifixion might be meant. The NIV probably

EZRA, NEHEMIAH, AND ESTHER

is correct in using the word *gallows*, since the word *gallows* is obviously used later in the story (5:14; 7:10).

Mordecai's name and the fact that he had warned the king are recorded in the book of the chronicles. This book is not either of the books of Chronicles that we have in the Bible. Rather, the book of the chronicles is the official daily record of the king's court.

❏ *Esther 3:1-15.* Just as Mordecai and Esther were introduced at 2:5-7, so now in 3:1 we meet the villain. Haman is introduced as the Agagite, that is, a descendant of Agag, king of Amalek. Saul had defeated Agag in battle, but he was also indirectly a part of Saul's downfall. Since Mordecai was descended from Kish (2:5), Saul's father (1 Samuel 9:1-2), Haman and Mordecai are enemies even before they meet.

For a reason that the author does not relate, King Xerxes promotes Haman to a position above all the princes. That is, Haman is now second in command in the kingdom. And at the king's command, all the people bow down and do obeisance to Haman. Everyone, that is, except Mordecai. Those who are at the king's gate with Mordecai ask him why he refuses to obey the king's command. He answers these people by telling them that he is a Jew.

It is not clear why being a Jew would prevent Mordecai from bowing before Haman. It cannot be claimed that Jews never bowed before kings, for that seems to have been common practice (1 Samuel 24:8; 2 Samuel 14:4; 1 Kings 1:16). The Additions to the Book of Esther, found in the Apocrypha, have Mordecai praying that he will bow down to no one but God. But the Hebrew text does not even hint that this is the reason. Similarly, the Targums (early Jewish commentaries) supposed that Haman had an idol embroidered on his robe, so that to bow down before him was to bow down before the idol. These are simply attempts to give a religious significance to Mordecai's act. But the truth of the matter is that the Bible gives no reason for Mordecai's refusal to bow before Haman. The only reason it even hints at is that Mordecai was a descendant of Kish, the father of Saul, and Haman was a descendant of Agag, a bitter enemy of Saul.

Haman is very angry when he learns that Mordecai will not bow down or do obeisance to him. He is so furious that he seeks a way to destroy all the Jews in the kingdom of Xerxes. First he has to discover which month and which day of the month would serve his purposes best. To do that "they cast the *pur* (that is, "the lot)" before Haman. We are not told who "they" are. As a matter of fact, the Hebrew is in the singular— "*he* cast *pur*." Obviously the *he* does not refer to Haman, since "he cast *pur* before Haman." Perhaps the pronoun refers to one of the wise men. The *pur* selects the thirteenth day of Adar, the twelfth month.

Next Haman must get the permission of the king for his intended slaughter. He does this by telling Xerxes that certain people in the kingdom have different laws from everyone else and do not obey the king's laws. Therefore, he concludes, the king should not tolerate them. Having laid out the problem, Haman now proposes his solution. He suggests to Xerxes that they be destroyed. Haman then offers to put a huge sum of money, "ten thousand talents of silver," into the king's treasury if the king would issue such a decree. By giving his signet ring to Haman, the king has given Haman the authority to write any decree he wishes and sign it with the king's seal. And the king's words to Haman show that is what he intended. "Do with the people as you please," he says. And he tells Haman to keep the money.

Haman then summons the king's secretaries and has them write an edict. The edict is written in the name of King Xerxes, sealed with the king's ring, and then sent by couriers to all the king's provinces. It decrees that the king's satraps, governors, and princes are to destroy, slay, and annihilate all Jews on the thirteenth day of the twelfth month.

The couriers hurry to deliver the edict. "The city of Susa was bewildered" at the decree. And that is probably putting it mildly. The people are shocked and horrified that such a thing should be done. In stark contrast, the king and Haman sit down to drink together.

DIMENSION THREE:
WHAT DOES THE BIBLE MEAN TO ME?

Should the Book of Esther Be in the Bible?

Reread the material at the beginning of this lesson. In light of these facts, do you think the Book of Esther should or should not be in the Bible? Why? When The Additions to the Book of Esther in the Apocrypha are included, the book becomes much more religious. Should we, then, accept these additions as part of the Book of Esther? Why or why not? Under what circumstances, if any, might a book be either added to or taken from the Bible? Of what lasting value is the message of Esther?

Esther 3:8—Treating People Who Are Different

Haman makes his case before Xerxes by pointing out that the Jews are different. Their "customs are different . . . and [they] do not obey the king's laws." Anti-Semitism has been encouraged throughout the centuries because the Jews have refused to be like everyone else. Other groups, too, have suffered the same fate. The Anabaptists, the Mormons, and the Jehovah's Witnesses have all been persecuted because they were different.

Why is it that we cannot tolerate differences? How would the world be different if everyone were just alike? How should we treat those who are different from us?

Esther 3:15—What a Contrast!

Whether intended or not, the contrast between the reaction of the city of Susa and that of the king and Haman is one of the most striking in all literature. This scenario has been compared to Nero's fiddling while Rome burned. It also brings to mind times in our own lives when we have callously passed by some need because either we did not realize how desperate the situation was, or at the time we did not care. Think about such situations in your life or in the life of someone close to you. If you can, share one or more experiences with the rest of the class. Looking back, how would you have acted differently?

ESTHER BECOMES QUEEN

*Haman went out that day happy
and in high spirits (5:9).*

—— 11 ——
Esther Plots
Against Haman
Esther 4–5

DIMENSION ONE:
WHAT DOES THE BIBLE SAY?

Answer these questions by reading Esther 4

1. What does Mordecai do when he learns about Haman's plan to destroy all the Jews? (4:1-2)

2. What does Esther do when she learns about Mordecai's wailing? (4:4-5)

3. What does Mordecai ask Esther to do? (4:8)

4. Why does Esther hesitate to approach the king? (4:10-11)

5. What warning does Mordecai send back to Esther? (4:13-14)

6. What challenge does Mordecai send to Esther in that same message? (4:14)

7. What message does Esther send to Mordecai in return? (4:15-16)

Answer these questions by reading Esther 5

8. What happens when Esther approaches the king? (5:1-3)

9. What does Esther request? (5:4)

10. What does Esther ask for when the king repeats his offer at the dinner? (5:5-8)

11. What turns Haman's joy into anger? (5:9)

12. What do Haman's wife and friends suggest to him? (5:14)

13. Does Haman have the gallows built? (5:14)

DIMENSION TWO:
WHAT DOES THE BIBLE MEAN?

□ *Esther 4:1-7.* When Mordecai learns of Haman's plan to annihilate all the Jews in the kingdom, he tears his clothes, and puts on a sackcloth and ashes. He then goes out into the city, and wails a loud and bitter cry. And wherever the Jews hear the king's decree, they mourn, fast, and weep. They also wear sackcloth and ashes. These, of course, are traditional signs of grief and mourning.

Esther's maids and eunuchs tell her that Mordecai and the Jews are all wailing, and she is deeply distressed. She wants to talk to Mordecai to find out what is going on, but he cannot enter the king's gate clothed in a sackcloth. So Esther sends clothes to Mordecai, so he will take off his sackcloth, but he will not accept the clothes. We are not told why he will not take off his sackcloth, but apparently it was because the matter is so grievous to him that he cannot yet stop mourning. Another reason could be that he wanted to let Esther know the seriousness of the situation. But he could have told her that personally if he had accepted the clothes and entered the king's gate.

He could also have refused the clothes because the situation causing the grief has not been cleared up yet. But he later appears without his sackcloth even though the matter is not yet settled. Or it might be because he wants to let Esther know this is not just a personal affair, but a public matter. His refusal of the garments would tell her that because the Jews are not supposed to make a public nuisance of themselves over personal grievances. But, again, he could have gotten this message to Esther by talking to her, and before this he had always had access to Esther by entering the king's gate. It seems best, therefore, to accept Mordecai's grief as genuine. He refuses the garments because he is still in mourning.

Since Mordecai would not come to her, Esther sends a messenger to him. Hathach is one of the king's eunuchs, who has been appointed to attend Esther. Mordecai tells Hathach everything that has happened to him, and he tells him about the money that Haman has promised to put into the king's treasuries for the destruction of the Jews. We are not told how Mordecai learns about the private conversation of the king. Perhaps he has an informer in the king's court, or perhaps he simply overheard some gossip that happens to be accurate. Mordecai also gives Hathach a copy of the decree. He wants Hathach to show it to Esther. He then tells Hathach to tell Esther to make supplication to the king to save her people.

But Esther is hesitant. Everyone knows, she says, that "for any man or woman who approaches the king in the inner court without being summoned the king has but one law: that he be put to death. The only exception to this is for the king to extend the gold scepter to him and spare his life" (4:11). Then she tells Hathach to tell Mordecai that she has not been called in to see the king for thirty days. Mordecai's answer is either harsh or full of practical wisdom, according to how it is interpreted. He tells her that just because she is in the king's palace, does not mean she will escape. Even if some of the Jews are saved, Esther will still be killed. Then, on a more positive note, he tells her that perhaps she was sent to the kingdom for just such a time as this.

Mordecai's message convinces Esther of what she must do. But first she needs the support of the people. She tells Mordecai through her messenger to gather all the Jews in Susa and hold a fast on her behalf for three days and nights. She says she and her maids will fast also. Then she will go to the king. Esther is very aware of the danger involved in going to the king without being summoned, but she decides to take the risk. "If I perish," she says, "I perish." Having received this message from Esther, Mordecai goes away and arranges the fast.

❏ *Esther 5:1-14.* The time for Esther to approach Xerxes has arrived. She puts on her royal robes and, according to the Old Latin version of the Bible, beautifies herself with ointment. Then she stands in the inner court of the king's palace and waits to be noticed by Xerxes. When the king sees Esther he is pleased and holds the golden scepter that was in his hand out to her. Esther approaches the king, and touches the top of his scepter. The king asks Esther what her request is. Xerxes must know the pounding that is in Esther's heart, for her very life has been on the line. He must know, too, that something very important is on her mind or she would not have taken such a chance. Perhaps as a way of relieving her anxiety, he assures her that her request will be taken care of, even if she wants half of his kingdom. The promise of "half the kingdom" is a common one in folk tales, but it hardly seems like a promise a real king would make (Mark 6:23.) It is commonplace to refer to this remark as a polite gesture, not to be taken seriously.

Esther is not ready to make her request yet. Instead, she asks only that the king and Haman come to a dinner that she has prepared for the king. When did Esther prepare any such dinner? While she was fasting? If so, the aroma must have been sorely tempting! The king agrees to the arrangement, and has Haman brought quickly. At the dinner, while they are drinking wine, the king repeats his offer to Esther. He wants to know what her request is. Xerxes knows that Esther has not made her real request yet. No one would endanger her life just to invite the king to a banquet. But Esther is still not ready to ask the king for her favor. Instead, she asks only that the king and Haman come to another banquet the next day. As Haman leaves the banquet, he is "happy and in high spirits"—happy, that is, until he sees Mordecai at the king's gate. Mordecai still will not pay Haman the respect Haman feels he deserves. This infuriates Haman.

When Haman gets home, he calls his friends and wife together and brags to them about his wealth, the number of his sons, and all the promotions that the king has honored him with. Then Haman adds that even Queen Esther invited only the king and himself to the banquet she prepared. He tells them that he has been invited by Queen Esther to another private banquet the next day. Haman obviously has no idea that Esther is working against him and his plan to exterminate all the Jews. As far as he knows, he is sitting on top of the world!

But then, there is Mordecai! When Haman thinks of him, his joy turns to wrath (verse 9). "But all this gives me no satisfaction," he says, "as long as I see that Jew Mordecai sitting at the king's gate." Haman's wife and friends suggest to him that he build a gallows that is seventy-five feet high, and in the morning tell the king to have Mordecai hanged. Then he can go with the king to dinner and be happy. This idea pleases Haman in spite of the fact that earlier he had "scorned the idea of killing only Mordecai" (3:6). Haman has the gallows made and is full of confidence that the king will grant his request.

DIMENSION THREE: WHAT DOES THE BIBLE MEAN TO ME?

Esther 4:11-16—Undaunted Discipleship

Esther has been criticized for her reluctance to appear before Xerxes without having been called to do so. She is accused of having more interest in her personal safety than in the welfare of her people. There may be some truth in that accusation, but how willing are we to risk our lives for others? How willing are we even to be inconvenienced for the sake of others?

Jesus said, "If anyone would come after me, he must deny himself and take up his cross and follow me" (Mark 8:34). Can we hear that? ". . . take up his cross and follow me." The cross is an instrument of death. Are we ready to die for others? Jesus did. And he also said, " 'No servant is greater than his master.' If they persecuted me, they will persecute you also" (John 15:20; see also Matthew 10:24 and John 13:16). What would it mean for your own life were you to become that kind of disciple?

Esther 5:11-13—This Does Me No Good

Poor Haman! He has great riches, a large number of sons, and has been promoted to second in command in the kingdom. He even has invitations to go with the king to a banquet to which no one else has been invited. "But," he says, "all this gives me no satisfaction as long as I see that Jew Mordecai sitting at the king's gate." Who do you know with a similar attitude? A thousand reasons to be happy, but we are so blinded by our one disappointment that we cannot see them! What would it take to make you really happy? Why?

Esther 5:14—"Merrily, Merrily on High!"

Haman's wife and friends had a very simple solution to his problem of despondency. "Have a gallows built, seventy-five feet high, and ask the king in the morning to have Mordecai hanged on it." After that, he can go to dinner with the king.

That uncomfortable solution sounds very much like the proposals we sometimes hear for solving some other problems. How many times have we heard people say—or have said ourselves—"There's nothing wrong with this company (or club, or union, or store, or church) that a few good funerals wouldn't cure." Do we realize what we are saying when we say that? Is that all there is to reconciliation? Is that why Jesus died on the cross? Is that what Paul has in mind when he says, "So in Christ we who are many form one body, and each member belongs to all the others" (Romans 12:5)? Let Mordecai swing from on high, and we shall go merrily on our way!

So they hanged Haman on the gallows
he had prepared for Mordecai (7:10).

— 12 —
Esther Intercedes
for Mordecai
Esther 6–7

DIMENSION ONE:
WHAT DOES THE BIBLE SAY?

Answer these questions by reading Esther 6

1. Why does the king have the book of the chronicles read to him? (6:1)

2. When the readers come to the place where it is written that Mordecai warned the king of the plot against his life, what does the king ask? (6:3)

3. When told that Mordecai has never been honored, whom does the king ask how he should be honored? (6:6)

4. Whom does Haman think the king wants to honor? (6:6)

5. What honor does Haman suggest? (6:7-9)

6. Whom does the king say is to be honored, and who is to lead him around the city? (6:10)

7. What do Haman's wife and friends tell Haman when they learn of his humiliation? (6:13)

Answer these questions by reading Esther 7

8. What does Xerxes ask Esther as he and Haman are dining with her? (7:2)

9. What petition does Esther make of the king? (7:3-4)

10. What does King Xerxes do when he learns that Haman is the one plotting to kill all the Jews? (7:7)

11. What does the king see as he returns to the banquet hall, and what does he think is happening? (7:8)

12. What order does Xerxes then give? (7:9-10)

DIMENSION TWO:
WHAT DOES THE BIBLE MEAN?

Last time we saw Haman honored by Esther, or so he thought, by being the only person invited to have a banquet with the king and queen. He relates all his good fortune to his wife and friends, only to end by saying, "All this gives me no satisfaction as long as I see that Jew Mordecai sitting at the king's gate." So Haman's wife Zeresh and his friends suggest that he have a gallows made, seventy-five feet high, and that he talk to the king the next morning about hanging Mordecai. This pleases Haman, and he has the gallows made. Today we continue that story by seeing what was going on with the king on that very same night.

❏ *Esther 6:1-14.* The king cannot sleep; so he has the book of the royal chronicles brought in and read to him. He has this particular book read to him either because he did not want to waste valuable time, or because he was restless and had to have something to occupy his attention, or because he thought the reading of such dull material would surely put him to sleep! When the person who is reading gets to the place where it is recorded that Mordecai has exposed the plot on the king's life, the king asks what honor or dignity has been bestowed on Mordecai for this action. He is told that nothing has been done for him and the king determines that something should be done. The king then wants to know who is in the court. He is looking for any high official who might be able to help him decide on an appropriate way to honor Mordecai. Only Haman is there, for it is very early in the morning. Even he would not have been there except for the fact that he has come early to talk to the king about having Mordecai hanged. The king has Haman come in.

The king asks Haman what he thinks should be done for a man the king wants to honor. Haman assumes the king is talking about him, so he proposes the most lavish honors he can think of. Let the man wear royal robes, he suggests, and not just any royal robes, but robes that the king has worn. And let the man ride on the horse that the king rides. The horse will even wear a royal crown. And let one of the king's most

ESTHER INTERCEDES FOR MORDECAI　　**93**

noble princes lead the man on horseback through the open square of the city. And let this prince announce to all, "This is what is done for the man the king delights to honor!"

These suggestions please the king. What nobler prince is there to lead the man around the city than Haman himself? So the king tells Haman to hurry and take the robes and the horse to Mordecai the Jew. And the king does not want Haman to leave out anything that Haman suggested. Poor Haman! He came to request that Mordecai be hanged, and he ends up proclaiming Mordecai's honor to everyone in the city.

After this humiliating experience, Haman hurries back to his house and covers his head and mourns. The covering of one's head or face is a sign of deep grief or shame (2 Samuel 15:30; 19:4; Jeremiah 14:3-4; Ezekiel 24:17). Haman tells his wife and friends about everything that has happened to him. But rather than words of sympathy, he receives an oracle of doom: "Since Mordecai, before whom your downfall started, is of Jewish origin, you cannot stand against him—you will surely come to ruin!" And while this conversation is still going on, the king's eunuchs come to take Haman to the banquet that Esther has prepared.

❏ *Esther 7:1-10.* On the second day of the banquet, after they had eaten and as they were drinking wine, the king asks Esther for the third time what her request is (5:3, 6). This time she is ready to tell him. "Grant me my life"—that is, don't let me be killed—and let my people be spared too. She goes on to say that the Jews have been sold. They are to be destroyed, to be slain, and to be annihilated. She would not even have bothered King Xerxes with this, she says, if the Jews had been sold merely into slavery, for then the affliction of the Jews could not compare with the loss to the king.

Some translations have Esther mentioning to Xerxes "the loss the king would suffer." What loss? Remember those ten thousand talents of silver Haman offered the king for the privilege of annihilating the Jewish people? (3:8-9.) As the text now stands, Xerxes does not accept Haman's money, but lets him do as he will to the Jews free of charge (3:11). But did the story say that originally? Many believe it did not. There are five considerations that point toward the conclusion that in the original version of the story, Xerxes accepts the money. (1) Refusing such a large amount of money just does not seem like what a king would do. Ten thousand talents of silver are not to be sneezed at, no matter how rich the king is! Someone has estimated the modern equivalent to be around fifty million dollars. (2) When Mordecai is in mourning, and sends a message to Esther by way of Hathach, he tells Esther "the exact amount of money Haman had promised to pay into the royal treasury for the destruction of the Jews" (4:6-7). There is nothing said here about the king's having refused it. Indeed, Mordecai's plea loses much of its force if the king had refused the money. Either Mordecai knows nothing of the king's refusal or else he is purposely deceiving Esther.

However, verse 4 of Chapter 7 seems to clinch the matter. (3) Esther says, "For I and my people have been sold for destruction and slaughter and annihilation." How are they sold if Xerxes did not accept the money? (4) If Xerxes refused the money, of what loss to the king is Esther speaking? It is hard to imagine what loss Esther is speaking of if she does not mean the ten thousand talents of silver. (5) If we assume that Xerxes accepted the money, that also clears up the matter of why Esther was so reluctant to make her request of him. She is asking him to give up fifty million dollars. And even now she endangers her life by asking, "I would have kept quiet," she says, if we were just talking about going into slavery. For, what is our slavery compared to ten thousand talents of silver for the king? But we are talking about our *lives!* "For I and my people have been sold for destruction and slaughter and annihilation."

The king is outraged. He wants to know who would presume to do something so terrible. Once again, Esther takes her life in her hands, for the man she is about to accuse is the second most powerful person in the kingdom. She cannot be sure at this point whether Xerxes will favor her over Haman, or Haman over her. But she has gone too far to turn back now. "The adversary and enemy" she cries out, "is this vile Haman!"

The king leaves the room in wrath. Haman is terrified and stays in the room to beg for Esther's mercy. And Esther apparently is reclining on the couch. She has been reclining on the couch as the customary way of dining at a banquet. Haman falls on the couch where Esther is in order to beg for his life. Xerxes returns to the banquet hall, and sees Haman on the couch with Esther. Seeing this, Xerxes assumes that Haman is assaulting the queen in his very own home. As soon as Xerxes cries out, the king's attendants, sensing that Haman's fate is sealed, cover Haman's face. By covering Haman's face, the eunuchs could be signaling that Haman is a condemned criminal.

Then Harbona, one of the eunuchs in attendance to the king, tells Xerxes about the gallows that Haman has had built for Mordecai. He reminds the king that Mordecai saved the king's life. "Hang him on it!" the king tells his attendants, and his command is obeyed. Haman is hanged. After that, "the king's fury subsided."

DIMENSION THREE:
WHAT DOES THE BIBLE MEAN TO ME?

Esther 6:6-11—Sealing Our Own Tomb

So sure was Haman that he was the one the king planned to honor that he suggested the highest honors he could think of. But this suggestion led to the deepest humiliation for him. When have your pride, your conceit, or your self-serving deeds ever backfired on you? What is the best way to handle a situation like that, when we are embarrassed beyond words?

Esther 7:4—How Much Is a Human Life Worth?

"If we had merely been sold as male and female slaves," says Esther, "I would have kept quiet, because no such distress would justify disturbing the king." That raises for us the question, How much is a human life worth? If you had it in your power to kill a whole people or to let them live, and you were offered fifty million dollars to have them all killed, what would you do? How would you justify your decision to those who thought you should have decided the other way?

Esther 7:9—A Loyal Servant or an Opportunist?

As soon as the tables began to turn against Haman, Harbona was ready to accuse him further. Why? Was he just being a loyal servant, or did he hope for some reward from the king? Harbona had done obeisance to Haman before (Esther 3:2). Did he secretly resent this, and wish for Haman's downfall?

And what about us? Do we enjoy it more when someone is cast down than we do when someone is lifted up? Why? How can we change our attitude about the unfortunate circumstances of persons we do not like?

Therefore these days were called
Purim, from the word pur *(9:26).*

— 13 —
The Feast of Purim
Esther 8–10

DIMENSION ONE:
WHAT DOES THE BIBLE SAY?

Answer these questions by reading Esther 8

1. What does the king give Esther, and what does he give Mordecai? (8:1-2)

2. What does Esther plead for from King Xerxes? (8:3-6)

3. What authority does Xerxes give Esther and Mordecai? (8:8)

4. What privilege does Mordecai grant the Jews in his letter? (8:10-12)

5. How do the people of Susa react when Mordecai walks among them? (8:15)

Answer these questions by reading Esther 9

6. What do the Jews do all the thirteenth day of Adar? (9:1-2)

7. Why do the nobles and satraps and other royal officials decide to help the Jews? (9:3)

8. How many men do the Jews slay in Susa on the thirteenth day of Adar? (9:6-10)

9. What does Esther now ask of Xerxes? (9:13)

10. Do the Jews of Susa continue to slay men on the fourteenth day of Adar? (9:15)

11. Do the Jews of other provinces of the kingdom slay men on the thirteenth of Adar? (9:16)

12. What do the Jews in the other provinces do on the fourteenth day of Adar? (9:17)

THE FEAST OF PURIM   **99**

13. When do the Jews in Susa rest and feast with joy? (9:18)

14. What does Mordecai instruct the Jews to do in a letter he writes? (9:20-22)

15. Why are the fourteenth and fifteenth days of Adar called Purim? (9:24-26)

Answer these questions by reading Esther 10

16. Where can more information about King Xerxes be found? (10:2)

17. Why is Mordecai popular among his fellow Jews? (10:3)

DIMENSION TWO:
WHAT DOES THE BIBLE MEAN?

❑ *Esther 8:1-17.* Justice would have been served had the story of Esther ended at 7:10. What follows is poetic justice, justice that goes beyond what one might reasonably expect. King Xerxes gives Queen Esther Haman's estate and he gives Mordecai the signet ring. The ring marks Mordecai as second in command in the entire kingdom. Then Esther makes Mordecai executor of Haman's estate. Thus, everything that Haman once had, Mordecai now has—he is next in rank to

King Xerxes (10:3), feared (9:3), famous (9:4), and powerful (9:4). He has control over vast fortunes (3:9, 5:11) and is able to write whatever he pleases, sign the king's name, and seal it with the king's ring (8:8). And besides all that, he has what Haman never had, the cheers and affection of the people (8:15, 10:3).

But though all this wealth has come to Esther and Mordecai, the edict of Haman to annihilate the Jews is still in effect. Esther, therefore, falls at the king's feet, and begs him with tears in her eyes to cancel Haman's order. But the king cannot, for once an edict is written in the name of the king and sealed with the king's ring it cannot be revoked. What he can do, however, is to allow Esther and Mordecai to write another edict, saying whatever they please with regard to the Jews.

Esther and Mordecai waste no time. They summon the king's secretaries on the twenty-third day of the third month, which is the month of Sivan. That is only two months and ten days after Haman's edict went out (3:12). The new edict goes to every official—satraps, governors, and princes—in all of the one hundred and twenty-seven provinces. It is also sent to the Jews. The edict is written to every province in its own script and sealed with the king's ring. The letters are carried by mounted couriers riding on swift horses that are bred from the royal stud. The edict states that the Jews are allowed to defend their lives, to destroy, slay, and annihilate any armed force of any people or province that might attack them. They may also plunder their attackers' goods on the thirteenth day of the month of Adar. This is the exact counterpart of the edict of Haman (3:13).

Then Mordecai goes out dressed in royal robes, golden crown, and a mantle of fine linen, and all the people of Susa shout and rejoice. And in every province and city the people are glad and there is joy among the Jews. And many of the native people declare themselves Jews because they are now afraid of the Jews. How different from the situation after Haman's edict went out (4:3)!

❑ *Esther 9:1-19.* The fateful day arrives. The people have an edict that cannot be revoked that says they are to slaughter the

Jews. And the Jews have an edict that cannot be revoked that says they are to defend themselves and to annihilate anyone who attacks them. What will happen? The Jews gather in their cities to await the attack of the Persians. But the people of Persia have lost their heart for the slaughter because they are afraid of the Jews, and they are not able to make a stand against them. The princes, satraps, governors, and royal officials also help the Jews because "the fear of Mordecai had seized them" too.

The Jews kill all of their enemies by slaughtering and destroying them. So complete is their victory that the Jews take the law into their own hands and do as they please to the people who hate them. In Susa the Jews kill five hundred men, and the ten sons of Haman. At this time they do not plunder the defeated enemies.

The victory seems complete. But the king wants to be sure Queen Esther is satisfied. "Now what is your petition?" he asks. Whatever it is, he will grant it for her. Esther replies, "If it pleases the king, give the Jews in Susa permission to carry out this day's edict tomorrow also, and let Haman's ten sons be hanged on gallows" (verse 13).

Esther's request raises some questions in our minds. If the victory was as complete as verses 2-10 indicate it was, what possible motive could Esther have other than a bloodthirsty desire for revenge? And what place does a desire such as that have in a book in the Bible? Furthermore, why should she request that Haman's ten sons be hanged on the gallows? According to verses 7-10, they already have been killed. What possible purpose could this serve, then, except for humiliation and to make them a public example? And again, what place do these motives have in a book of the Bible?

But the king sees no problem with Esther's request. He commands this to be done. The ten sons of Haman are hanged and the Jews who are in Susa gather on the fourteenth day of Adar, too. Once again there is a slaughter. The Jews kill three hundred men in Susa. And once again, we are told that "they did not lay their hands on the plunder."

The other Jews, that is, those in other parts of the empire, also gather to defend their lives and their property. They, too, experience great victory. They slay seventy-five thousand people who hated them. But like their city compatriots, they also laid no hands on the plunder. (Perhaps this phrase is repeated so often to emphasize that the Jews are killing these people for moral reasons, not material gain.)

For the Jews in the provinces there was only one day of battle, since it was only the Jews in Susa who fought on the thirteenth and the fourteenth days. The Jews in the king's provinces fight on the thirteenth day and then on the fourteenth day they rest and make that a day of feasting and gladness. Since the Jews who were in Susa fought on both the thirteenth and the fourteenth, they rest on the fifteenth day, making that their day of feasting and gladness. That explains why the festival of Purim is two days and why the Jews of the villages celebrate the fourteenth day of the month of Adar as a special day of gladness and feasting, while the Jews of Susa hold their day of gladness and feasting on the fifteenth.

❑ *Esther 9:20-32.* The rest of Chapter 9 is concerned primarily with the establishment of Purim. The author's purpose no longer seems to be to tell an interesting story. It is rather to prove that Purim is a legitimate festival and should be observed by all Jews. Because of this shift of emphasis, some have thought that 9:20-32 is written by a different author.

The author recognizes that the festival arose spontaneously. The words *they had begun* in verse 23 would indicate this realization. But shortly thereafter, Mordecai made the festival legal, binding, and permanent. This legalization took place in three stages: (1) Mordecai's letter establishing the festival as a two-day affair (verses 20-22); (2) the Jews' declaration that they would "without fail observe these two days" (verses 23, 27-28); (3) the letter from Esther and Mordecai confirming the festival (verses 29-32).

❑ *Esther 10:1-3.* The book closes with a tribute to Mordecai, but in proper fashion also acknowledges the greatness of King Xerxes. Also included is one new item of information—the king levied a new tax on the people (verse 1).

THE FEAST OF PURIM   **103**

DIMENSION THREE:
WHAT DOES THE BIBLE MEAN TO ME?

Esther 9:13—Getting Even Is Never Enough

Haman's edict in 3:13 is distressing to read. That one would seek "to destroy, kill and annihilate all the Jews—young and old, women and little children" is a horrible idea. But it is equally distressing to read Mordecai's edict in 8:11, and equally horrifying to think the Jews should seek "to destroy, kill and annihilate any armed force . . . that might attack them," and that includes their children and women. This is pure revenge, "eye for eye, tooth for tooth" (Exodus 21:23-25; Leviticus 24:19-20; Deuteronomy 19:21; Matthew 5:38). Worse still is Esther's request in 9:13. She is not satisfied that the Jews have slaughtered thousands of people throughout the empire. She wants a chance to do the same thing again tomorrow! Where is the spirit of love, of kindness, of forgiveness? Is it too much to expect the heroes and heroines of the biblical stories to have compassion?

How should we, as followers of Christ, react when we are wronged by someone? Should we expect the same kind of action from Esther that we expect from Christians? Why or why not? Do you normally act more like Jesus or like Esther?

Esther 9:1—Unconscious Influence

The leader's guide points out in the discussion of 9:1 that the only enemy of the Jews we hear about before 8:13 is Haman (3:10; 7:6; 8:1). Beginning in 8:13 and continuing throughout Chapter 9, the Jews suddenly have a lot of enemies (9:5, 16, 22). Why? What has caused this shift in attitude toward the Jews? Is it possible that Haman's attitude has spread to other people?

How likely is it that you and I will be influenced by the views of those around us? How likely is it that we shall influence others? Can these influences occur even when we are not conscious of them? When have you influenced someone without being aware of it? When has someone influenced you without you being aware of it?

Esther 10:3—Power, Corruption, and the Shield of Faith

You are familiar with Lord Acton's famous expression, "Power tends to corrupt and absolute power corrupts absolutely." Acton's words are not absolutely true. For only God has absolute power, and "God is love" (1 John 4:8). On a human level, however, Acton's words have proved to be distressingly true time and time again. But look at 10:3! Here we find a man who has risen to second in command in the kingdom, and who "became more and more powerful" (9:4), yet he "worked for the good of his people and spoke up for the welfare of all the Jews."

What persons do you know who have risen to places of power, yet who have managed to stay humble? What persons have you thought power would never corrupt, but apparently it has?

About the Writer

The writer of these lessons on Ezra, Nehemiah, and Esther is Dr. Brady Whitehead, Jr. Dr. Whitehead teaches at Lambuth College, Jackson, Tennessee, and is an ordained United Methodist minister. He is a member of the Memphis Annnual Conference.